Discovering
My Gypsy Soul

Discovering My Gypsy Soul

Catina Borgmann

Discovering My Gypsy Soul by Catina Borgmann

Published by GypsyWander
www.GypsyWander.life

Copyright © 2023 by Catina Borgmann

For permissions, contact: hello@gypsywander.life

Cover by David Provolo

ISBN: 979-8-9872321-0-1 (print)
ISBN: 979-8-9872321-1-8 (eBook)

Printed in the United States of America

Contents

Introduction

Driving and listening to music are two of my favorite things. A song I've heard many times before, "Colder Weather" by Zac Brown Band, came on during one of my drives. I have a particular affinity for this song because it refers to a truck stop diner just outside of Lincoln. I was sure it was the Shoemaker's truck stop outside my hometown of Lincoln, Nebraska. I would see this place in my mind whenever I heard the song. I could picture the night as black as the coffee he was drinking. I was disappointed to learn it was actually a truck stop in Lincoln, Montana.

But on this particular day, it was not the truck stop diner outside Lincoln that caught my ear. It was a lyric: "got a gypsy soul to blame, and you were born for leavin'." The song kept playing, but it was in the background while this line repeated over and over in my mind: a *gypsy soul to blame, and you were born for leaving.* That lyric resonated deep within me. A gypsy soul—I was so drawn to this and wanted to know what it meant. Born for leaving—maybe that's what the unsettled feeling is that keeps coming back after I've been someplace for a while.

I've been antsy and restless lately, feeling so unsettled. I'm not sure why, but it's a feeling I get that seems to be on a cycle, although I haven't figured out the timing of that cycle yet. I want to do something or go somewhere or be something—a craving for something to change. To tide myself over for a bit, I decided to paint my front door a bold color. That might satisfy my craving for the short term, but it's like a snack to someone who really wants the whole buffet.

While sensibly I want clarity, consistency, and stability, I seem to thrive in the midst of uncertainty, variation, disorder, and chaos! During these times of uncertainty, I feel most motivated, ambitious, and alive. I feel more driven, like I have a purpose. These times captivate my attention, and I feel involved in my life.

So, how do I find a balance? What is the compromise? I want the security of being stable, but at the same time, I crave the wildness and wonder of this unpredictable world! I long for the adventure and excitement of unfamiliar places and experiences. I aspire to understand the inner workings of our hearts and minds. I yearn for a spiritual experience with God's creation that is outside of routine life. I want a life I love, a place to play, and room to roam.

Too much routine makes me bored and anxious. Of course, we are creatures of habit, so I appreciate a certain amount of consistency in my life. I generally keep a pretty normal bedtime, wake time, and mealtime, and I need frequent downtime away from people to recharge. These things in my life stay pretty consistent, but beyond that, I get the same feeling as someone who is claustrophobic entering a small space: riddled with anxiety and panic. Those feelings don't go away quickly. "Antsy" is the best way to describe it, but it's more severe than that. It can sometimes be intense, and there is a definite backlash from having these yearnings.

Throughout this book, I'll discuss some of the reactions I've received based on different choices I've made. I've spent so much of my lifetime telling myself to settle down and that these feelings will pass. At other times, I've worked hard to stuff my feelings down and convince myself it's not normal to want these things—

or at least not normal to act on them. I should be happy to settle in and find comfort in the predictable, but the annual vacation to wherever doesn't satisfy me like it does others.

I Googled "What is a gypsy soul?" when I got home from that drive. I found a sweeping description of myself! Different characterizations were given depending on the source, but they all echoed traits I am familiar with. The descriptions were a complete embodiment of my feelings, my strengths, my characteristics, and my personality. I had just seen a reflection of myself, though I was not in front of a mirror.

This was one explanation from the Urban Dictionary: Someone who possesses a gypsy soul is a person always in need of change and/or adventure. A gypsy soul seeks the next best thing in any life situation. They can be very passionate and are often inspired by different ideas, attitudes, and experiences. Their sense of identity doesn't always make clear what they want out of life, but they are determined to find it.[1]

What? You can easily replace the subject in all those sentences with my name! "Catina possesses a gypsy soul and is always in need of change and/or adventure. Catina seeks the next best thing in any life situation. Catina can be very passionate and is often inspired by different ideas, attitudes, and experiences. Catina's sense of identity doesn't always make clear what she wants out of life, but she is determined to find it."

That, my friends, is who I am! That is what feels true and right. That is who God created me to be. I am embracing it, and this insight is essential to me finding my purpose!

My early childhood into adulthood consisted of great confusion, mystery, adversity, and struggle. Is that why today I seek change

---

1 Wolfskill, "gypsy soul," in the Urban Dictionary, August 16, 2021, accessed August 10, 2022, https://www.urbandictionary.com/ define.php?term=gypsy%20soul/.

and adventure? Is that why I'm always searching for something new and different? Or maybe running away from everyday life became a coping mechanism I learned and developed to survive in the world? Or maybe, just maybe, these are all just parts of me—the *real* me, the me that I was created to be. I suppose the answers to some of these questions may become clear as I continue defining what it means for me to be a gypsy soul.

Do you have this hankering for adventure too? Then come with me down this unknown path of discovering if you too have a gypsy soul.

Latcho drom!
(LAH-cho DROM, "Good journey," the traditional Romani farewell.)

1

"Everything you can imagine is real."

−Pablo Picasso

Discovering My Gypsy Soul

There are hundreds of articles touting, "Ten things you need to know if you are a gypsy soul," or "These are the signs you have a gypsy soul," or "How do you know if you have a gypsy soul?", all with lists of character traits that a gypsy soul embodies. Of course, everyone has a unique perspective, but the ideas in these articles are pretty consistent. Taking into account their similarities, I compiled and condensed the statements from these lists. I want to explore each component individually and in greater detail. Through my journey, you might find what you need to give yourself the necessary hope and determination to achieve your own self-actualization.

These are the elements I will explore:

- You are an old soul in a modern world.

- You are self-sufficient, unpredictable, and fiercely independent.

- You are not scared of life, and life doesn't scare you.

- You are a collector of moments; material things are not important.

- You are a passionate person who asks deep questions and thinks on the deeper aspects of life.

- You love nature and art. You are imaginative and creative. Music runs through your veins.

- You let your emotions guide you. You are empathetic. You trust your intuition.

- You believe in magic and miracles. You are optimistic and know something good is always around the corner.

- You dance to the beat of your own drum and live an unconventional lifestyle. You're constantly looking for something new and exciting.

- You are a free-spirited, adventurous wanderer who loves your freedom.

● You are full of energy and want to live life on your own terms, always open to change and embracing chaos. You have fire in your soul.

● You are afraid to fall in love, but you love unconditionally.

I found myself excited to get home from the part-time merchandising job I picked up for the summer and fall so that I could start writing. I couldn't wait to explore this concept of being a gypsy soul. It was a new idea to me, but it seems like something I should have known all along!

You know how whenever you learn an unfamiliar word or consider buying a particular car, you start hearing that word or seeing that vehicle everywhere? That is happening to me now with the word *gypsy*. I hear that word in so many songs, from Cher and Bonnie Raitt to Fleetwood Mac and Shakira, Jimi Hendrix and Bob Dylan to Eric Clapton and Van Morrison. I hear all the songs that have references to gypsies. My antenna is up and laser-focused, so I notice it all the time.

I just returned from a trip to Tulum, Mexico, with my friend. One of the very first things I saw as we explored the area was a shop displaying a book called *Tulum Gypset*. I immediately wondered if *gypset* was a version of the word *gypsy*, so of course I Googled it. Turns out *gypset* is a term coined by author Julia Chaplin, combining the word *gypsy* with *jet set*. How ironic! I guess the universe was telling me I was on the right path with this gypsy soul idea.

In those first days of writing, thoughts and ideas constantly swirled through my mind. I would write down keywords from my thoughts, hoping that by the time I was able to write again, I would remember what I'd thought when I jotted the word down.

Gypsy (capitalized, or the politically correct term, *Roma*) refers to a member of a people originating in South Asia and traditionally having an itinerant way of life, living widely dispersed across Europe and North and South America and speaking a language (Romani) that is related to Hindi.[2]

The term *Gypsy* has a negative connotation attached to it. A stereotype of the Gypsy people is that they were/are prone to stealing. The derogatory slang term *gypped* comes from this stereotype and means someone has ripped you off or cheated you. Culture has labeled Gypsies as lower class, dirty, deceitful, and too lazy to work. They were and still are widely misunderstood. People assumed they were from Egypt because of their dark complexions; that is how they became known as Gypsies. But they actually originate in northern India. The Romani people have a nomadic way of life and move from place to place, which seems mysterious and suspicious to other people.

The term *gypsy soul*, on the other hand, has become an expression of the self, an identity—a way to describe how someone thinks, feels, and acts, including their personality and overall nature. It means a person who is prone to wander and just can't seem to stay put, or someone who always needs change or adventure. At a high level, that is definitely me. This just might be the piece of my puzzle I have been missing. So, instead of running from my natural inclinations, I am committed to embracing who I am and choosing a path that makes me happy.

---

2 Google Dictionary, s.v. "gypsy," accessed October 31, 2022.

2

"She's an old soul with a kind
of spirit that can't be tamed.
Let her be free, let her run,
let her live."
−Madiha

You are an old soul in a modern world.

Daughter, sister, Christian, niece, mother, friend, neighbor… Confident, decisive, intense, competitive, ambitious, persuasive… So many words can be used to describe who or what we are.

I've had friends refer to me as an "old soul," but it never meant much. I'm not even sure how I would define the term if someone asked me to. Maybe someone who seems wiser than others their age? Or someone who has a taste for vintage items or likes history? I wonder what comes up if you Google "old soul"?

According to Dictionary.com, an old soul is a person, especially a child or young person, who demonstrates a maturity, understanding, or seriousness that is typical of someone much older.[3] Let's get Webster's opinion… What? Webster doesn't even list the word! Maybe I am just plain old! Why wouldn't Webster have this term in the dictionary? I guess I will go to Wikipedia, which passes me off to Wiktionary. That makes sense; we wouldn't look in an encyclopedia for a definition. (If you don't know what an encyclopedia is, look it up on Wiktionary!) Wiktionary defines an old soul as "a reincarnated person" and "a person of unusual maturity."[4]

Google proves useless in this situation. If Google were sarcastic, it would have said an old soul doesn't use Google to define things! Let me provide a more complete description based on my research. An old soul can be described as someone who is wise beyond their years and feels deeply connected to things of old or to the past. They may sometimes feel like an outsider, especially as a child who is more mature than their peers. They are introspective, spiritual, and reflective.

I can see why some say gypsy souls are old souls. I identify as an old soul based on this definition. As a child, I was always mature for my age, and I have a fascination with history, especially ancestry. I feel there are connections between ourselves and the family members that came before us, much more than we tend to think about. Can you imagine sitting down with your great-great-grandparents for a conversation? What would you ask them? What commonalities do you suppose there are between you and your relatives who lived four generations before? We don't usually wonder about our ancestors' personalities, but try to for a moment. When you close your eyes, can you feel them in your heart? If you follow your heart,

---

3 Google Dictionary, s.v. "old soul," accessed August 17, 2022, https://www.dictionary.com/browse/old-soul/.

4 Wikipedia, s.v. "old soul," accessed August 17, 2022, https://en.wiktionary.org/wiki/old_soul/.

do they appear on your path? What if you have a personality just like your great-great-grandmother? What if she was a gypsy soul too, and that is what she passed down to you? Wondering about this makes me excited and motivates me to continue discovering myself. I want to carry a torch for future generations. I may have a great-great-granddaughter someday who reflects on me, wondering if I gave her my gypsy soul.

How do you suppose future generations will learn about us? The 1950 census was recently released, and you see a lot of television commercials for Ancestry.com. They say, "Learn more about what your family's world was like in 1950." It's interesting information about a generation that didn't have Facebook and Twitter to post life updates and memes. Maybe when they release the census for the year 2000, it will be a nonevent. People will have already scrolled through the Facebook timelines of those they want to learn more about. It does make you think about the legacy you are leaving behind. Surely, they will wonder what the fascination was with taking pictures of our food, won't they?

I remember riding home in the backseat of the car when I was probably eight years old.

My favorite TV show at the time was *Little House on the Prairie*. I wanted to be Laura Ingalls; I loved her spunky personality and wanted to be just like her, out there adventuring on the wide-open prairie. I must have fallen asleep in the car and started dreaming while my dad was driving. I dreamed that life alternated every other year between present-day times and what I refer to as the "olden days." During the even years, we had cars to drive and all the modern conveniences. In the odd years, cars disappeared, and we were back to horses and buggies. One year, you would be in third grade with other third graders, and the next, everyone attended a one-room school with all the grades together. We went from wearing shorts and T-shirts back to dresses and boots. I was heartbroken when I woke up and asked when it would be time to go back to the olden days, and my parents looked at me like I was crazy. It was almost like the Cinderella story; everything would switch when the clock struck midnight on the last day of the year. My dream was so real, and I wanted it to be a reality! I wanted to live like Laura.

Several years ago, I visited some real-life Laura Ingalls Wilder locations. I quickly realized I was more a fan of the television show than of the real-life Laura. Seeing the actual places didn't give me the same images I was anticipating.

⟋

Throughout my life, my friends have generally been older than me. I never planned it that way; that's just how it happened. I felt I had more in common with girls who were older than me. They were more mature, like me. They were interested in things that interested me. We had conversations about life and more important things than fashion and boys. I could create a deeper connection with people older than me than I could with my peers. I found myself wanting to scream, "Grow up!" to my classmates many, many times. I didn't, of course; I was more mature than that!

⟋

When I was growing up, history was boring and irrelevant to me. Kind of ironic for someone who dreamed of living in the olden days! Today, history fascinates and intrigues me. I was fortunate enough to travel to Israel in November 2016 on a pilgrimage to the Holy Land. Talk about the ultimate history field trip! To be where Jesus was during his time on earth, to walk where he walked, to see and feel the lay of the land... It was an incredible experience. While on a boat ride on the Sea of Galilee, I expected to look up and see Jesus walking on the water!

One of my favorite experiences while there was visiting the village of Magdala, home of Mary Magdalene. Jesus visited Magdala often and taught in the synagogue there. It has only been uncovered recently, but it is absolutely magnificent to see and walk in this place. As I listened to our guide tell us about the discovery of the synagogue, I walked along its contours, staring, imagining, and feeling Jesus there at that moment, and I became emotional. I couldn't hold back the tears rolling down my face. Jesus—my Jesus—was *here*! He had walked in this exact place; he taught here and lived part of his human life here in this very place.

A mosaic still covers a large part of the original floor, all these tiny tiles side by side, making perfect lines in the design, unlevel now from the earth settling beneath them. The tiles are so tightly connected that they have moved along the dimples of the earth the mosaic was created on. It almost looked more like a rug than a mosaic! I then came to a section of the wall that had been painted in what was likely a red rectangle with a yellow border outlined by thin black lines. I imagine farther up, in the red portion, had been some picture in the center, but that part of the wall was gone. Such a vivid red and yellow! Wow—paint? I never thought of people painting in Jesus's time, but certainly the synagogue would have been beautiful and ornate, full of color. I wondered what they might have made paint from in that time and reveled in how the color remained today after being hidden under the earth for all those years.

I turned around, facing toward the village and seeing this

bustling city come to life in my mind with all the remnants of what had been uncovered. Suddenly, the time and distance between now and then, here and home, evaporated. I wasn't looking at a replica or a model; I was actually there! Profound energy flowed through my body and surrounded me. I was in awe.

This is only one story, but these are the experiences I crave—something so deep you can barely put it into words.

My aunt didn't have any children of her own, and my brother and I were the only kids in the family.

She would always take us to fun places, like the Kansas City Renaissance Festival in Bonner Springs, Kansas. I loved going each time. I have been to a few other renaissance festivals over the years in various locations, but this one is by far the best and most realistic. It was like visiting a magical place in history. The characters, the costumes, the way they talked, the man-powered rides, the comedy skits with audience participation, the Royal Court Parade, the jousting…

The festival goes on rain or shine. One year, it rained off and on the entire time we were there, but we still had a blast. It just added to the fun. At the end of the day, I was the only one who hadn't slipped and fallen. As I walked proudly toward the exit to the parking lot, my gloating ended as I went down. Now, I was not only wet and muddy, but I had to ride home like that! Everyone else had fallen earlier in the day and had the chance for their clothes to dry.

The first year that we went, there was a structure fashioned as a medieval jail or dungeon. It was one of the first places to stop after you entered, and I vividly recall it. Inside, they had all these actual torture devices from medieval times they told us about. Let me tell you, those people found some of the most bizarre ways to torture a person, and for some insane reasons. When we returned in later years, there was no longer a medieval jail to visit. I'm sure they shut down the display for liability reasons, along with their gruesome descriptions. By no means am I a person fascinated with torture, and I don't know why this is such a crystal-clear memory, but being immersed in the culture from this time period was so captivating! As an adult, I took my own kids to the festival for several years. They found the same joy I had in being there.

I am an old soul in a modern world.

3

"A bird sitting on a tree is never afraid
of the branch breaking,
because her trust is not on the branch
but on its own wings.
Always believe in yourself."

–Charlie Wardle

You are self-sufficient, unpredictable, and fiercely independent.

Being self-sufficient, unpredictable, and fiercely independent is like getting all sevens on a slot machine: jackpot, in my opinion. Others would say it's being bullheaded, obstinate, stubborn, or headstrong. I call it the way God made me. We all know someone who is self-sufficient or unpredictable or independent, but what about a person who is all three wrapped into one?

Since I strongly exhibit all those traits, I think it's the jackpot.

When I try to manage more than I should, I will hear someone say, "Here, let me help you," to which I will respond, "No, thanks, I got it." I would be moving, and neighbors would offer to help, but I would say, "I should be able to get it myself."

I made up my mind that I was picking the blue paint for the living room. When it was painted, someone would say, "I thought you were going with yellow?" I simply changed my mind at the last minute.

I like to think I don't need anyone, for anything, ever. I can do it myself—until I can't, or until I can't keep pretending I can. I want to appear capable, as if I don't struggle. I want everyone to think I have it all together, all the time. But how realistic is that? We all struggle, and God created us for community. He created us to need other people, to be in relationship with one another. I know this, I believe this, but I struggle with this. My deep-seated conviction is still that I can do it all myself.

Being self-sufficient is not necessarily a bad thing. I'm competent and don't need outside help in taking care of myself, or need anyone to provide for me. I am a childhood abuse survivor, and I know this has influenced my self-sufficiency. I've experienced unbalanced give-and-take during my life, so my instinct is to figure it out on my own. Self-reliance is all I've known.

Being independent—even fiercely independent—is not necessarily bad either, although it's usually a defense mechanism from constantly being let down. I believe in my own strength, and I am skillful, resourceful, and tenacious. I find it difficult to ask for help—painfully difficult. I don't want to burden anyone or ask somebody to go out of their way just to help me. Plus, if I don't ask for help, I can't be disappointed, and I can avoid feeling like I owe someone.

I've always been the helper, never the help-ee. I don't want to be judged as needy, criticized for needing help, or blamed for why I needed help. I would have to give up my perceived control to ask for help, which is something I don't generally allow myself to risk. I know this is an unhealthy view. But believe it or not, I have worked on this and gotten better. I still have a long way to go though!

Unpredictability can be enjoyable, especially when you revel in change. Flexibility is necessary if you are an unpredictable person. You have to be able to go with the flow and not get caught up in every detail. My unpredictability can also show up in my emotions, which is not so enjoyable. I can be happy and sociable one minute, then feel depressed and detached and need my own space to recharge the next. It's not only an outward unpredictability, it's inward too. I can be as confused as you are about a shift in my emotions, so I'm always trying to find something that can heal my heart. It's a lifelong journey.

People are not naturally self-sufficient and independent. We are born into the world completely dependent and cannot care for ourselves in any form. Although I hear it's not done anymore, doctors used to spank newborn babies to even get them to start breathing on their own! Life skills are taught or learned and developed out of necessity or survival.

When an adult is extremely self-sufficient and independent, it's likely a trauma response. I know childhood trauma is what forced me to perfect these characteristics in myself. They served me well for many years—so many that they became ingrained into my identity. I don't know how to *not* be self-sufficient and independent. When someone grows up experiencing trauma, they are usually isolated from others who can support them, so they endure the abuse and aftermath alone. This creates terrible loneliness and isolation. But to be alone or isolated signals that the abuse has ended, at least for the moment.

This is true for me. Even today, I automatically retreat into isolation to feel safe. I don't even realize I am doing this, but when I am stressed out or confused, I tend to want to be alone and have no contact with anyone—just me and my own safe little world. I think this is where my preference for small spaces came from too. In a defined space, I feel like I have control.

~~~~~

I've been single and living alone for many years. There's not much I won't try to do by myself. When I was living in Lincoln, Nebraska, I lived in an area called Woods Park. It was full of big 100-year-old oak trees that dropped debris year-round: leaves, acorns, or catkins, constantly clogging my gutters. I lived in a one-and-a-half-story house, so my gutters were high enough that I needed a ladder to clean them. Being afraid of heights, I would try everything I could to clean them out from the ground. My family was always willing to come help, but it had to be done so frequently that I felt I needed to figure out how to do it myself.

Eventually, I found a great tool you can screw onto your garden hose. It had a hook that would go into the gutter and spray everything out. In theory, at least, that was how it was supposed to work. When I hooked the tool over the gutter and turned the water on, the connection between the hose and the tool was right at my head. The connection was not sealed properly, so water sprayed in my face. I fixed that issue and tried again. For an instant, it worked like a charm. Then, as I moved down the gutter, the connection to the hose would twist, and water would start spraying me in the face again. I quit turning off the water to tighten it and just kept going. Finally, I had moved all the debris through one section of the gutter, but it wouldn't flow through the downspout. Instead, the gutter filled with water and began overflowing on my head. Can you picture me? I was drenched from head to toe and had gutter crap stuck to my arms and face! I tried and tried. I wanted to do it myself. I finally gave up and felt so defeated that I just wanted to cry. I turned off the water and went inside to take a shower.

When I was looking for a house, I wanted to buy a fixer-upper, something I could live in and continue working on over the years. I had a budget and am somewhat handy, or at least willing to learn. The more I could do myself, the better. But finding something in my price range was difficult at the time. Inventory was sparse, and it was a seller's market. No one could have predicted what would happen next: I bought a house posted on Craigslist. Yes, Craigslist! It was a fixer-upper, for sure. It had no electricity, no plumbing, and no drywall, the floors had been stripped down to the original floorboards, and when you stood in the living room, you could look up and see the plywood sheeting of the roof. It was basically a brick shell that had been completely gutted. The roof was new, so it did have one positive feature! This wasn't quite the fixer-upper I'd originally had in mind. It was a bit more extreme, but it was an experience and an adventure.

I loved that house and watching it become the creation I en-visioned. I couldn't do the work myself, but living through the unpredictable design and construction stages generated some of my best memories (and biggest frustrations!) When I purchased the house, I had been living in a third-floor apartment in an area that made me question my safety. I was tired of the noise, the frequent visits from the police to my downstairs neighbors for domestic disputes, and all the Walmart carts that would end up in the apartment complex parking lot. All this was a lot, and I was ready to get out of there, so I did.

Remember, my house was a shell with no plumbing or electricity—but I did have a driveway. So, I lived at my newly purchased home in my vehicle while it was being remodeled. Yes, really. Eventually, my contractors put in a temporary toilet and shower for me, and at a certain point in the construction process, I could "move in" to an area in the basement and sleep in a bed. It was an experience that still brings a smile to my face.

~

Gypsy souls are fiercely independent, self-sufficient, and unpredictable, taking responsibility for their own lives and happiness. Some of us may have become like this because it was who we needed to be to survive, but those skills have also helped us thrive throughout adulthood. I've always said to leave things better than you found them, whether people or places. I am no exception to this rule.

I am self-sufficient, unpredictable, and fiercely independent.

4

"Twenty years from now you will be
more disappointed
by the things that you didn't do
than by the ones you did do.
So throw off the bowlines, sail away
from safe harbor.
Catch the trade winds in your sails.
Explore. Dream. Discover."
—Mark Twain

You are not scared of life, and life doesn't scare you.

I grew up in a small town in Nebraska—ridiculously small, with just 423 people at the time. My family lived in the same house for my entire childhood. A few times, my parents considered moving, not far away, but to a different, more suitable house, closer to my dad's job. I was thrilled by this idea for many reasons. I couldn't wait to start over in a new house. I remember in one potential house I had even picked out my bedroom. It was a multilevel house, and my bedroom would be the one another girl already occupied. It had a yellow canopy bed, just like I'd always wanted. It was right at the top of the stairs, and I could see myself there. The possibilities were so exciting.

We never did end up moving, which was disappointing. I wasn't scared at the thought of having to start over at a different school or make new friends. Even at an early age, I craved change and had a desire to try new things!

It wasn't until I was a young adult and my dad passed away that my mom moved from the small town to the city. If my dad had continued living, they would still be there today; I'm sure of it. They were content to stay put in the same place forever. That is where they had built their lives. I've never understood the need or desire to stay in one place. In many ways, staying gives you consistency, security, and a comfort zone that is supposed to be highly desirable. People are supposed to strive for the American dream: a good job, a house with a white picket fence, marriage, and kids. Once you achieve the highly sought-after American dream, well, there isn't any expectation after that. Congratulations: you won.

There is nothing wrong with wanting to live in the same place for your whole life. I would even say most people from Nebraska are born and raised, work, live, and die in the same town and are very happy doing so. That is their comfort zone, and they have no desire to seek anything different. Why fix something that isn't broken?

I, however, am not one of those people.

After high school, I was enrolled to attend nursing school away from home, but I decided to stay close because I had a boyfriend I didn't want to leave. So, I moved into the city the weekend after I graduated from high school, and I enrolled at a local nursing school, but they had a waiting list. My name came to the top of the list the week my dad was diagnosed with cancer, so I had them put me back on the bottom of the list.

In the meantime, I got married and landed a decent job, so I forwent college. Over the next several years, I had two babies and basically achieved the American dream. I did what was culturally acceptable and followed the unspoken rules. I was happy with the life prescribed to me. My itch for adventure and change was temporarily satisfied by moving my family into different homes. I also held a leadership position in a professional organization, so I traveled to various conferences throughout the year, which helped.

Even so, I was caught up in the "I'll be happy when…" game. "I'll be happy when I have a bigger house; I'll be happy when I have a yard; I'll be happy when I get divorced; I'll be happy when I have a boyfriend; I'll be happy when my kids are older; I'll be happy when…" Fill in the blank.

By 2015, I had been divorced for ten years and hadn't been in any sort of relationship for over three of them. I had wanted to visit a state park in Illinois for nearly five years, but I was waiting for someone to go with me. I asked my friends, my kids, and my family. No one was interested, so I waited. Someday I would find someone adventurous who wanted to travel with me.

The desire to go waxed and waned for years, but suddenly, on a random Wednesday evening in September, the door to my cage opened, and I started to become free. I was sitting in my living room scrolling through Illinois' Starved Rock State Park website on my phone, dreaming of someday—someday when I had someone to go with me—when I had an epiphany. The thought entered my head so clearly: *What are you waiting for? You can go by yourself!*

Even thinking back on this moment, it was utterly surreal, a thought so powerful and yet so simple. Why hadn't I thought of this before? Perhaps it just hadn't been time for me to break out of the cage I had been living in. The wheels in my mind started turning immediately. I wasn't waiting around for my mind to change or convince me I was crazy to think I could do this alone. I wasn't waiting to be scared or decide I shouldn't or couldn't do this. In fact, I wasn't scared at all, even though conventional thinking would suggest I should be.

Instead, I sprang into action. No thinking, just doing. I went downstairs and dragged my IKEA twin-sized mattress up the stairs and out to my Chevy Trailblazer SUV. I was fairly sure it would fit in the back with the second-row seats folded down. It fit like a glove. Perfect! I own a tax business, so since it was September, I was flexible as far as work went, and my kids were at their dad's. I grabbed some hiking clothes and other necessities, tossed them in the back of my SUV, and headed to my usual Bible study on Wednesday nights. Afterward, I filled up on gas and posted on Facebook that I was running away. I headed east toward Illinois at 8:30 p.m. on this random Wednesday night! I was ecstatic and so full of energy. I drove through the night, listening to music that sounded more amazing than it ever had before. I sang so loud and danced around in my seat. I felt so free, so excited, so liberated!

I drove until about 2:30 a.m., when I pulled into a Walmart

parking lot. I'd heard about other people spending the night here, usually with a camper. I found a space near a light, climbed in the back, and tried to go to sleep. I was tired and needed to quit driving, but sleep—I just couldn't! There was so much excitement inside, and all these unfamiliar sounds outside. I felt like people were parking next to me, even though they were not when I popped my head up to check. And the light! I felt like parking next to a light was the safe thing to do, but how do you sleep with so much light pouring through your windows? I dozed off briefly a few times, never going fully to sleep. I rested my body as best I could between the noise, the light, and my excitement. Around 6:00 a.m., I gave up trying to sleep and drove to a nearby gas station to use the bathroom and get coffee. I got back on the road as the sun was rising and drove for another couple hours before arriving at Starved Rock State Park in Oglesby, Illinois, at about 9:30 that morning. The lack of sleep started settling in, but my excitement carried me on.

Along one of the trails I hiked, I found a bench, where I sat and pulled out a notebook. I needed to get all these thoughts swirling around in my head out on paper. Then an older gentleman walked by and struck up a conversation with me. He was a widower and had been to Starved Rock many times since his wife had passed. He told me stories of the many trips he and his wife had taken over the years. They were travelers, and it had taken him a good bit before he was comfortable traveling again without her. I told him this was my first time traveling alone and how this trip had come to be. He commented on the freedom that both traveling and getting out in nature provides. His words encouraged me to think beyond this one adventure to a future of traveling, with or without someone. As he continued on his journey, I continued to write and think about possibilities. I wish I could tell that man today how much he impacted me and how that short conversation with him changed the whole course of my life.

I had an article saved from Facebook that was shared many times in 2015. It was a post about a Michigan State University doctoral student who used an algorithm to create the most efficient route across the forty-eight contiguous US states, making a stop at a national monument, landmark, park, or noteworthy site in each state.[5] I wasn't sure of my reason for saving the article at the time, but I remembered it while I was sitting on the bench. And my mind started imagining, *I could do that*. After all, I had gone to Illinois alone; why couldn't I travel across the United States by myself? Part of me felt like I was just exercising my imagination, but another part of me was completely serious and planning a real-life adventure. I studied the map. If I did this, I would be leaving from Nebraska. Where would I start the route? Would I travel the route clockwise or counterclockwise? What stops are along the way? Thoughts continued pouring into my head, and I had to get up and move so I could process all these ideas. My excitement started to grow as I began to realize this was no exercise of my imagination, but an actual adventure I was going to embark on!

The thought of traveling solo never scared me. I never even thought about being scared—not until others would ask, "Won't you be scared?" or "Is that safe (and smart) to do?" or "A single woman traveling in her vehicle alone—that's a pretty crazy idea!" Others were envious, saying they wished they could do that or be so brave. It had never dawned on me that what I was planning to do was brave, or could be scary or unsafe. I only thought about freedom and adventure. I was finally living the life I had put on hold while waiting for someone to travel with.

5 Randal Olson, "Computing the optimal road trip across the U.S.," March 9, 2015, https://randalolson.com/2015/03/08/computing-the-optimal-road-trip-across-the-u-s/.

I set out on this adventure on April 29, 2016, just after tax season ended. I had a three-ring binder with my tentative route that I had researched extensively, and that same IKEA twin-sized mattress in the back of my SUV. I didn't know how long I would be gone. I guessed two months, but I wasn't tied to my route or a calendar. I was ultimately away for eighty days and 13,454 miles. I traveled everywhere east of Colorado. During those eighty days, I spent fourteen nights in hotels, nine nights with friends or family, and the rest in my vehicle.

When you travel solo, being totally responsible for yourself, you will inevitably discover just how capable you are. It took me a couple days to feel at ease. I remember having to get used to making every decision myself. There was no one to ask, "Should we do this or do that?" I couldn't say, "Whatever you want to do is fine with me." I'm so passive in those areas that it was an adjustment for me to make all the decisions in every situation.

The trip was life-changing. I can honestly say there was only one time that I was scared. I wasn't in danger, but I was so far outside my comfort zone that I felt scared. These feelings came from being unprepared.

I had originally planned to spend about three days in Montreal, Canada. My initial preparation for getting into Canada was entering Quebec through Vermont and going straight up to Montreal. My research suggested it is a friendly city, easy to get around in, and even though it is a French-speaking area, most everyone speaks English too. I didn't think much about it; after all, I was only going about two hours north of the States. How different could it be? But I was very wrong.

I had changed my route, so I entered Canada by way of Ontario from New York instead. At first, this was exciting—all the different road signs in French and English, and the speed limit in the metric system! I had to use the alternative numbers on my speedometer for kilometers per hour.

Then I entered Quebec, the land of all things French. Instantly, I felt like a foreigner. Suddenly my comfort of signs in both French and English was stripped away. Everything was in French—no English anywhere. It was obvious what some of the road signs were, but not all of them, and there was road construction the closer I got to Montreal. There were lots of flashing signs, but I had no idea what they were warning me of.

Typically, I tried to arrive in any new city by late afternoon. This gave me time to get acquainted with where I was and figure out where I was going to park and stay for the night, all during daylight. But I had been delayed at the border. (For your own travels, just know that bringing mace into Canada is illegal!) This delay caused me to get into Montreal at dusk. On top of this, navigating a new city—heck, a new *country*, with different laws and weird street names so long I had a tough time remembering them until I passed my turns—made this arrival unnerving. The lanes were narrow, people drove fast, and many of the roadways merged into one lane. Maybe the signs said that, but I couldn't read them if they did. I'm not sure if it was due to construction or just how the streets are, but many lanes were not marked. They had green flashing lights. What do you do when you see a green flashing light? I'm sure I stuck out like a sore thumb with my Nebraska license plates.

There were so many tunnels, and when I went through the first one, I immediately thought of the pictures from the news of Princess Diana's crash. I just needed to get out of that tunnel and find somewhere to stay for the night and come up with a plan. I generally parked for the night in hotel parking lots. I soon found a hotel but had no idea what part of town I was in or if it was safe. So, I opted to get a room for the night. I needed to plan, to calm down, and I knew getting a good night's rest would do me well.

Once morning came, I headed down to old Montreal, laughing all the way. GPS doesn't have a French accent, so it was pretty comical to hear the street names! Most street names were exceptionally long and very French. The one I laughed at most was the street named De Carrie. In your best French accent, how would you pronounce that? GPS pronounced it "Daycare-E," in the most American voice possible.

I found a metered parking space and pulled in. I looked at the meter, hoping I could make sense of it. I had no idea what parking times were allowed or how long I could park there. I'm sure Google Translate was available at this time, but I didn't know about it then. So, I put some American coins in and prayed my car would be there when I returned.

For my next stop, there was a parking lot with a pay kiosk. This was a little foreign to me, but how hard could it be? I was at the kiosk when a woman across the lot started yelling at me and waving something in the air. I had no idea what she was saying, and she sounded urgent, or maybe angry; I couldn't tell. I thought I must have parked in her space, or that the lot was not for public parking. As she got closer, I was concerned. I said, "English?" She smiled and said she had paid to park for the full day, and that I could use her ticket so I didn't have to pay. I accepted the ticket and thanked her. As I started to walk away, she stopped me and said I needed to place the ticket on my dash. Oh—duh! She giggled as we both walked back to our cars. I'm sure she thought I was a crazy American. The joys of being ignorant.

I had a wonderful day, visiting beautiful places like the Notre Dame Basilica, but it was clear I was not prepared for my visit. I had no Canadian currency and felt the stress of not being ready for this culture shock. I needed to find something to eat and just wanted to sit down and get my bearings. Many of the restaurants had menus posted outside. To an American, everything seems expensive when there are commas in the prices instead of decimals! I soon found a McDonald's and went in. There was no counter; you had to order from screens in the middle of the lobby. It was really busy, and I felt intimidated, so I left. Even though the menus were in French, there were pictures, so I certainly could have figured it out. But this was my first time going to a foreign country alone, and I was overwhelmed!

I had a headache and was mentally exhausted. This was my signal that my comfort zone had been sufficiently stretched. I decided I would visit again when I was more prepared and decided to head back to the US. I soon made it through the border and entered Vermont. I imagine my feelings about being back in familiar territory are similar to what a soldier feels when returning home. I wanted to get out of my car and kiss the ground!

I am definitely more prepared these days if I visit a foreign country. You live and you learn.

It might sound cliché, but I'm not scared of being scared. Being scared is okay. It stretches you and requires you to live in faith. We tend to avoid fear and not allow ourselves to experience it because feeling scared can be extremely uncomfortable. But being scared is a part of living, growing, and learning.

I am not scared of life, and life doesn't scare me.

5

"I don't care much for things that
I can't take with me after I die.
Give me love. Moments. Purpose.
Things that'll settle in the soul."
—A.R. Lucas

You are a collector of moments; material things are not important.

A collector of moments, yes; this most definitely describes me. I want experiences, not things. Whoever came up with the phrase "Who-ever dies with the most toys wins" had to be someone who profited from selling said toys. We live in a consumer society, bombarded with covert sales pitches. So often, we don't even notice when we're being sold to. The phrase "keeping up with the Joneses" originated as a comic strip in 1913, created by Arthur R. "Pop" Momand. Over a hundred years later, people are still trying to keep up. It will not stop on its own; marketers and advertisers make too much money convincing us that we need this or that.

I feel fortunate to be a person who doesn't get attached to physical things. Instead, I get attached to people and moments in time. There is not one material thing I would be tempted to save from a fire. Of course, that may be since photos are mostly digital now; otherwise, I might say photo albums. But you still don't need pictures to enjoy memories.

———

Christmas is one holiday among many that our country and the world have commercialized. I used to get caught up in the whole Christmas spending thing, and I still do sometimes, but I try to at least be more mindful of it. I keep a spreadsheet of gifts I purchase for Christmas as a planning tool. Some may say it's because I'm a nerd; I'm okay with that reason too.

In 2017, I was planning for an upcoming Christmas and looked at what I'd bought my kids the year before. There were some expensive items on there that they had asked for. As an experiment, I asked my kids what they remembered getting for Christmas the previous year. Neither had an answer—except for the case of gum I buy for them each year at Sam's Club! I let them think about it for a while, and still, neither could remember a single thing. I then prompted them from my spreadsheet. (To be honest, I couldn't recall anything without that list either.) "Oh, yeah, I remember now!" they responded. It's terrible that we spend all this money on gifts that we can't even remember nine months later! I resolved that this wouldn't happen anymore. Think about your own life; do you remember what you got as a gift last Christmas? Today, when I buy a gift, it must meet one of three criteria: it must be consumable, create a memory, or bring lasting joy.

That first Christmas after setting my gift criteria, I went big! I took my kids on a cruise; that most definitely hit the "create a memory" criterion. Making it even more memorable, my parents came along. (My mom remarried after my dad passed.) We made so many precious memories, and still today, we tell stories from that trip. My kids were extremely satisfied with the gift I chose and welcomed the idea of a vacation the following year. That hasn't happened again, but I know it will someday. When I ask them, even years later, what they got for Christmas that year, they remember. Not only were they happy, but it made my heart happy too. As a bonus, spending time with your adult or nearly adult children and seeing how wonderful they turned out is a blessing.

The Christmas after I moved to North Carolina, I wanted to do something special and unique for Christmas, since I was no longer living near my kids. I came up with an idea I have used ever since, and my kids look forward to it each year. I purchased an over-the-door shoe holder for each of them. I then filled each of the twenty-four pockets with a wrapped gift they could open each day of December, mostly consumable items—soap, a gift card for gas or groceries, beef jerky, toothbrushes, shampoo, etc. The idea has evolved since that first year.

Neither uses the shoe holder anymore to hold their gifts; actually, my son uses it for shoes now! It makes it easier not to feel like I need to limit myself to gifts that fit into the pockets. Now they get a box of gifts all wrapped in the same paper, a different paper for each kid, and each is numbered one through twenty-four. Previously, I would do more inexpensive, consumable gifts for the first twenty-four days and a larger gift for Christmas day. Now I give them some larger gifts throughout the month, generally timed to be opened on a weekend or closer to Christmas. Sometimes they open a picture of the item, and then have to go to my parents to pick it up!

They still enjoy getting household necessities, since few young adults want to spend their money on deodorant or dish soap! I made the mistake last year of not buying them dental floss toothpicks. They were both so disappointed and said they looked forward to getting those each year. Now they lamented about having to buy them for themselves! You better believe they are getting them this year—on three different days! I guess those toothpicks, along with the case of gum, are things they expect from me every year. I love that!

Throughout the year, I find gifts to use for the coming Christmas. It helps spread out the expense over the year. I'm always looking for something special for them and have so much fun with this Christmas tradition. I love getting their text messages with a picture of what they opened that day, what they guessed it was going to be, or how excited they were about a particular item.

Things are just things, and every *thing* can be replaced. It's people, relationships, and experiences that can't be replaced, and the memories created with those people or by those experiences will always be cherished over physical items. I'm grateful that I don't get attached to things, because I know many people struggle with this.

As I shuffled through boxes preparing for my move to North Carolina, I looked through one with items my son had saved. I think he saved a plastic cup from every place we've ever gone, but I also found one flip-flop. I asked if he knew what had happened to the other one. He said he did; he lost it in Texas at Schlitterbahn Waterpark. Puzzled, I asked why he kept the flip-flop if it didn't have a match. He said that when he saw that one flip-flop, he remembered how he lost the match. I was still puzzled, but now amused. I asked if he needed to keep that one flip-flop so he could remember the story, or if he could relive the moment without the visual reminder. He chuckled and threw the flip-flop in the trash.

We keep a lot of things just because it seems like a good idea at the time. That's how we ended up with a self-storage industry with annual revenues of almost forty billion dollars. I venture to guess most people with storage units don't even have a good recollection of what they have in storage, and could probably repurchase most of these items if they needed them with the money they would save each year on paying rental fees. If you don't have a rented storage unit, you might have a basement, an attic, or a closet full of things you have kept around in case you need them someday.

The Swedish have a phenomenal tradition called the Swedish Death Cleaning. It may sound morbid, but it is something you do before death. It's a practice of slowly decluttering your house so your death isn't such a burden on those you leave behind. I think it's one of the most caring and honorable things someone can do for their family. No one wants to go through a house full of someone's belongings after they pass. When you do something like a Swedish Death Cleaning, you are essentially taking responsibility for yourself and your own clutter instead of leaving it for someone else to take care of.

I limited myself to only what would fit in my Trailblazer when I moved from Nebraska to North Carolina. It was stuffed to the gills, but everything else was gone. I moved out of a 1,700-square-foot house full of furniture, décor, and stuff! It was also full of memories. Those memories I still have today. I don't need to be physically at that house or look at pictures to recall those memories; they are safely tucked away in my heart and mind. The memories I might have temporarily forgotten reemerge when I reminisce with my kids, family, or friends. Those are the treasures I take with me!

Sentimental items or items passed down from generation to generation can be the hardest things to part with. I get that. I have struggled with that too. When I was downsizing to what I could fit in my vehicle, I had many things I had to sit with for a while. For example, I had an old trunk my parents bought at an auction for me when I was in high school. They refurbished it inside and out. I used to keep all my important things in it—but I wasn't going to be able to take the trunk with me.

I have before-and-after pictures of the trunk, and memories of my parents proudly showing me the trunk when they brought it home. They said they bought it for me, and I was less than thrilled. An old, dirty, smelly trunk! Why did they think I wanted that? But their gift was beautiful, and something I treasured for many years when they were finished refurbishing it. I still treasure it in my memory. Keeping it would have only weighed me down. I no longer needed it; it was not something I would pass down to my children, since they weren't interested. I didn't need to physically see it to remember it, although I do have pictures if I want to look at those. It's the stories and feelings that are important to me, and I still have those.

Something I used to keep in my trunk was my dad's Bible, after he passed away. It was the Bible he received at his confirmation with his name engraved on it. It was something physical of my dad's that I could hang on to—but it wasn't my dad. From the time I had it in my possession, it just remained in that trunk. I would only see it if I opened the trunk, which wasn't often, and it didn't make me think of my dad or feel closer to him. Nonetheless, how do you get rid of a Bible? I had collected several Bibles over time: the one I received for my own confirmation, a Bible that belonged to my aunt who had passed away, and a Precious Moments Bible in pristine condition that I had gotten as a child. None of these Bibles were used anymore; they just took up space and gathered dust. I had my preferred Bibles that I used regularly.

Again, I would think, how do you get rid of a Bible? Do you donate it to Goodwill? That seemed inappropriate for some reason. I asked my pastor, who confessed he had never been asked that question. He said occasionally they gave "used" Bibles to people who participated in a prison ministry, but generally they gave them a new Bible of their own. In the US, we are fortunate to be able to easily acquire Bibles. These also had names inscribed on them, so it felt even more odd to use them for this purpose.

I did some research and found an organization called Love Packages. They do international mission work, sending the gospel to the ends of the earth by putting donated bibles and other Christian literature into the hands of people around the world. This is how you regift Bibles—and what a purpose-driven gift! So, I asked if others had Bibles they wanted to get rid of and told them where they would go. I ended up with a full box to send to Love Packages.

Months later, I received an email from them telling me the

cargo box of these donated Bibles was headed to Thailand. Somewhere in Thailand, there's someone reading my dad's Bible with his name inscribed on the front: Donald R. Borgmann. My dad was a man of great faith, and I know he would approve of the mission of Love Packages. The person with his Bible in their hands has no idea who my dad is or was, but they now know Jesus because of him! What an awesome way to memorialize my dad.

~~~~~

Recently, my uncle moved from Nebraska to Idaho. Years before, he had inherited a dining room set from my childhood home after my dad passed and my mom moved. The set had been a fixture of my childhood that my parents had inherited from my dad and uncle's grandparents. There are many memories of family holiday dinners around that table. Memories of the metal circle and string you would pull to release the latch, expanding the table to fit the leaves, making the table larger. Memories of the extra leaves that permanently lived in the closet of my childhood bedroom. Memories of the chairs my mom had recovered many times over the years to match the current décor. Memories of the matching buffet that had a perfect space for me to lay under and create my own little space when I was just a small girl. I can picture it all in my mind and remember seeing pictures of me when I was under the buffet with my blankets, tucked safely against the wall and behind the bars that ran between the buffet legs. Even then, I preferred small spaces; they made me feel safe and enclosed.

I saw pictures on Facebook of that old, sturdy table and buffet when my uncle was getting ready to move. I hadn't seen it in years, but even without pictures, I could instantly recall it from memory. No one wanted it anymore; after all, it was old and out of style, as it had belonged to my great grandparents. Passing down furniture from previous generations doesn't have the appeal it once did. Regardless of whether it was made into firewood or hauled off to the dump, it doesn't matter. I still have that old table and buffet and always will, in my memories.

I am a collector of moments; material things are not important to me.

6

"I like stormy nights and full moons.
I like wolves and wild water.
I like to wander and I like adventure.
I like unpredictable kisses and
conversations full of unexpected truth.
I like things that have soul.
They make me feel free."
—Brooke Hampton

You are a passionate person who asks deep questions and thinks on the deeper aspects of life.

I disdain small talk. I would rather skip the pleasantries and get right down to it. I'm really not interested in the weather. I feel no need to ask, "How are you?" to people who are only going to respond with the obligatory "Fine." My time is precious, your time is precious; let's just cut to the chase.

Sound too harsh? Maybe. But if you want to know how I really feel, there it is!

I know small talk is an icebreaker, a nicety, a way to enter into conversation, an olive branch to find common ground and interest, and necessary if you are going to meet people. But I want to get past the small talk to get to the good stuff.

What is this "good stuff" I'm referring to? Deep, thought-provoking conversation, where we can be vulnerable and share our opinions, thoughts, memories, and ideas about life, death, living, dying, struggles, triumphs, insecurities, God, dreams, fears, the future, the past, the present—things that really matter. Teach me something; tell me about your life experiences and the lessons you've learned. Give me authenticity!

I am a curious person. My mind is always churning, and I am relentless in questioning. If I'm watching a movie, I seem to have a question right before they answer it. I am sometimes just a step ahead of where I should be. I'm too impatient to let the story play out and wait for the questions to be answered. I want to skip ahead to the good stuff!

Curiosity can be a weakness, especially when paired with my inability to remain patient or quiet. Curiosity is a strong desire to know or learn something, and sometimes that desire makes me impatient, because I want to know it now! Alternatively, it also makes me adaptable, and if I work on the patience part, I can make curiosity the strength it is meant to be.

I'm open-minded, so I don't want to prove an opinion I've already decided on, but I'm earnestly looking for alternatives to my thinking. I am genuinely interested in people's ideas and perspectives, especially when they differ from mine. My mind is active, and I like to ask questions and search for answers. I'm thirsty for knowledge and understanding.

I remember in my thirties learning what "420" refers to: international pot-smoking time. I couldn't believe I had never heard that before, but I wasn't a pot-smoker either, so why would I have known? I had so many questions about this. The funny thing is that the first question I asked was if the time zone mattered! I was curious, and who knew when that information would be important? It turns out it is 4:20 a.m. or p.m. in whatever time zone you are in.

～

I attended a function last night hosted by My Neighbor's Voice (myneighborsvoice.org), an organization recently formed by two local women in Travelers Rest, South Carolina. I wasn't sure what exactly I was attending, but I thought the event might be interesting, and I was not disappointed. I was invigorated by the deep conversations I had with complete strangers! It's a phenomenal idea—dare I say movement to listen, love, and act as a community that shares stories and perspectives that offer hope. Its mission is to create purposeful and productive community connections. Using a moderated format, they provide a safe and hospitable space in which everyone is invited to share their personal stories, thoughts, and opinions about how to best live together. It's through deeply listening that we deeply connect, and when we are connected, we are resilient.

I know I was led to this group for a more significant reason. I will be learning more about the organization in the coming months, but this was my happy place as someone passionate about deep conversations about life. At the event I attended, there were only six participants and a moderator. They had rules—easy ones—to ensure that everyone had the opportunity to share their feelings and thoughts without fear of being interrupted or judged. Going in a circle, the first person chose a listening card from various topics, some political in nature, others about society, the world, sacred thoughts, or even yourself. When it was your turn, you picked a category to choose a card from. You could skip the card and choose another if the first card made you uncomfortable. You then had three minutes to share your thoughts and opinions about the particular idea on the card. There was no follow-up after your time ended; the cards were simply passed to the next person, and we continued. I was amazed at how freeing it was to simply listen. Since you knew you would not have to respond, you didn't have to think about your own opinions on the topic; you were free to just listen and absorb. I heard funny stories, heart-warming stories, emotional stories, ideas I had never con-sidered before, and opinions and viewpoints that I could hear and truly consider. We did four rounds of this, since there were just seven of us.

After the event, we all commented on our experience that eve-ning. Everyone felt it was beneficial and was glad they had partic-ipated. We even agreed that we started to feel connected to one another by the time we were on our third and fourth rounds. It was getting difficult not to comment or ask questions, but not be-ing able to do so was also the magic of the evening. We started to feel safe with each other, and the answers seemed to get a little deep-er, revealing a bit more of who we are and what we think. We were learning how similar we are and where we have our differences.

We felt okay to express those differences, knowing we could all remain calm and friendly, and respectful of someone who thinks differently than we do!

———

If I had the choice of sitting alone or making small talk with someone, I would choose alone every time. But have you ever met a person and you just clicked with them? You could talk for hours, and the conversations flow naturally. I love when that happens. I am at my best when I'm with someone where we can follow an intellectual trail and let it lead us where it may. Being vulnerable and having a philosophical debate is one way we make sense of things, form our opinions, and expand our values and minds.

I've learned to see a lesson in every situation. When you look at situations like this, things don't affect you the way they used to. You begin to grow through everything you experience. You start to shift your energy to create what you want, and you stop worrying about what you can't control.

———

I'm known in my family for a couple of unusual things.

Remember when we used to get new phone books delivered to our front doors every year? I used to remember what time of year that was, but not anymore. I knew the time of year because, for me, it was like getting the new Sears Wish Book! Yes, I was excited to get a new phone book every year. My family would tease me for "reading" the phone book—but do you know how much useful information was in there? And yes, some information would change from year to year. It was like what the ultimate community Facebook page would be today.

The other thing I am known for is reading the manual. I read all the manuals for all the things, really. The most useful one is and always has been the car manual. I believe that eighty-five percent of people do not use their vehicles to their full potential. Your car does so much more than you realize. You would know what I am talking about if you read your car manual.

<hr />

I tend to ask lots of questions in conversation. I am a good listener, but my curiosity makes me want to know more, in more detail, as you tell your story. I try to work on this; I know some people feel interrupted when I ask questions while they are speaking. But I want to dive deeper into topics. I want all the details. I am an information gatherer. This information helps me to understand, to generate theories and ideas. I not only learn about you, but I learn about myself in the process. So many times, talking with different people has helped me put words to something I couldn't describe, or given me a proper perspective on or understanding of a situation.

Sometimes I think of questions no one else has ever asked. Sometimes I find my own answers. Sometimes I help others to find theirs.

<hr />

Many years ago, before I realized how useful a car manual was, we were having problems with the transmission in our minivan. It was shortly after my dad passed away, and I had never taken a vehicle to a repair shop, because he was a mechanic. I was so scared to trust someone else with my vehicle and figured they wouldn't be able to help me, or that they would rip me off because I was young and a woman. I had to muster up the courage and blink away the tears forming in my eyes as I pulled into the shop. I told myself I could do this; I just needed to sound confident.

As I described what was happening with the vehicle, I referred to the prindle. The technician looked confused, or maybe he was just concerned about my issue; I didn't know, but I continued. When I finished telling him about the problem, he apologized and said he didn't know what a prindle was. And my immediate thought was, *I knew it. They can't help me, they don't know how to fix my car, and they don't even know what a prindle is. This was a waste of time; I just want Dad to fix my car.*

The shop was near my mom's house, so I walked there after I left my car to be repaired. When I told my mom they didn't even know what a prindle was, she smiled and said, "You didn't say that, did you?" Of course I did. How else could I tell them about the problem? This is an example of a time that I was not curious enough. I never questioned what a prindle was or why it was called that. I learned for the first time that day that there is no such thing as a prindle. It's just an acronym for "park, reverse, neutral, drive, low": PRNDL.

Why had no one let me in on the joke?

———

Have you ever been exposed to something that fascinates you or that you quickly developed a passion for, and you wanted to learn as much about it as possible?

When I was probably twelve years old, a family in our town had a house fire. In my small town, you would put flyers in the window at the grocery store to make announcements, and I saw a sign from the family who'd had the fire requesting help with cleanup on a particular weekend. I asked my dad if we could help them. At the time, I wasn't necessarily friends with the girl who lived there; I just felt the urge to help them, and everyone knows everyone in a small town. I couldn't imagine having to try to salvage things from your house after a fire; it made me really sad.

So, my dad and I helped during the weekend cleanup, and I was fascinated to see what the fire had done—the way the phone had melted right into the wall, the bathroom mirror had cracked from the heat, and decorative candles had melted into shapes I had never seen before. Some things were relatively untouched by the fire, even though they were right near something else the fire had destroyed. I'd had no idea of the damage a fire could cause or the things that could melt, and seeing this both fascinated and frightened me.

Fire is one of my worst fears. I have never personally been affected by a fire, and no one was hurt in the fire we were helping to clean up after, but I imagine that is where my fear came from. Because of this fear, I had a panic attack in the first house we purchased before our son was born. I was standing in the doorway between the kitchen and a stair landing when I smelled smoke. I knew there was a fire inside that wall. In fact, the fire my dad and I helped clean up after was an electrical fire that started in a wall. My husband tried to calm me down, but the more he tried, the more panicked I became. I was distraught because he wasn't doing anything, and I was sure there was a fire inside our wall.

I don't remember calming down, but I obviously did. I don't know what I was smelling or why I was convinced there was something on fire at that particular moment. I've never had a similar situation since, but fire is still both a fear and a fascination for me. Learning about fire, how it works, and the damage it causes is something I remain curious about.

I am a passionate person who asks deep questions and thinks on the deeper aspects of life.

7

"Creativity is seeing what others see and thinking what no one else ever thought."
—Albert Einstein

You love nature and art. You are imaginative and creative. Music runs through your veins.

Several years ago, I came across an event teaching fused glass art. I felt it was something I was skilled enough to handle. I sometimes overestimate my creativity and artistic ability, ending up with Pinterest fails rather than art, but this appeared to be foolproof!

I had so much fun making and arranging glass shapes I had cut, using glass rods, and sprinkling frit to create what I thought was pretty. I even experimented with a print transfer, where you can print something on special printer paper and it becomes part of a glass plate during the firing process. For one project, I duplicated the tattoo on my shoulder, and it's the one piece I still have today. It's a circular flat plate with the words, *Everything happens for a reason, just believe...* circling the outside edge. In the middle are three butterflies, one yellow, one teal, and one purple. The glass I used for the plate was flesh-colored, so it matched my tattoo almost exactly. It's special to me because the words are something my dad would say when he was dying and we were struggling to understand why his life was being cut so short, with him dying at age forty-seven.

I eventually moved into learning how to make stained glass and even tried blowing glass. Glassblowing, while fun, is challenging. Those attempts mostly turned into fails, but I look at them as one-of-a-kind Christmas ornaments. I still have a couple that haven't broken.

I've tried out most of the creative outlets over the years: the wine-and-painting thing, making a chunky blanket crocheted with my arms, scrapbooking, painting ceramics, cross-stitching, and diamond painting. I enjoy the process, but since I don't get attached to things and am not a collector of stuff, it becomes more about the experience and the memory. Once, I did a resin art class where we made a charcuterie board. We poured food-grade resin on a cutting board to make a design with whatever colors we chose. It turned out really well and is something useful too. But I enjoy writing most of all, and since that doesn't take up physical space, I tend to stick with that!

Nature never ceases to amaze me. In 2016, while on my road trip, I visited the Green Mountains near Stowe, Vermont. I drove through Smugglers' Notch, which had views beyond anything I ever imagined could exist. It was the first time I had seen such a landscape, and I immediately fell in love. I would pull my car over whenever I could; it was a narrow road that twisted and turned through massive rock formations. At one turnoff, I stopped to explore, immediately getting lost in time. I went on an expedition around these towering shapes, pressing my hand against them while I walked their outline. They were a majestic, peaceful green, with moss woven between them. I have a fascination with moss that might have begun there.

During this expedition, I happened upon a tiny stream that trailed down from above, through the rock and over the moss, disappearing next to the roadside, surely continuing downward. The sound was stilling. If I had to detail what the Garden of Eden was like, that is what I would describe. Even though I was there, touching the landscape, I wanted to be closer. I remember looking at how each individual rock was resting against the earth below, and I tried to envision the moment it came to rest in that exact spot. It had been in motion at one time and then came to rest in that very spot, in that exact position, creating that exact view of itself.

The shadows of each distinctive mass as the sun shone against them made the temperature stunningly different while I walked. I would feel the warmth of the sun, and then in my next step, feel the cool air radiating from the mound towering next to me. I could stay there, taking it all in, becoming part of this magnificent, heavenly place, but I became aware of the fact that I was feeling more chilly air than warm, and I realized the sun was setting. I didn't want to drive the trek down the mountain in the dark, so I vowed to return someday to explore further.

When I returned home from that road trip, having been to

so many unique and beautiful places, I designated this the most beautiful place I had been during those eighty days.

⁓

Music can make you happy, soothe a broken heart, cause you to break into spontaneous dance, excite you, motivate you, make you cry, take you back to a different place or time, remind you of a person or relationship, and heal you—or me, at least! Music is medicinal for me. It can instantly produce deep feelings.

I am not a musician—I'm not even a karaoke singer—but I am a consumer of music. What kind of music do I like? The kind you can hear. Every genre of music serves its purpose—yes, even the loud, screaming, can't-understand-what-they're-saying kind of music.

Have you ever watched a scary movie and been scared? Or a sad movie and become sad? Try watching a particularly scary or sad part of that movie on mute. Somehow it becomes boring, or even funny. If you feel scared or sad while watching it on mute, you've probably watched the movie too many times and can hear the music in your head. Often, we don't even register the music in movies that is inciting us to feel scared or sad, but without that soundtrack, feelings are lost or ineffective. Music makes us feel.

Watching live music is my favorite pastime—especially if some sort of drinking is involved! Sometimes I just like the tune, melody, or beat of a song (don't ask me to distinguish between those terms), and other times it's purely lyrical. I look up the lyrics to songs *all the time*! Admittedly, I sometimes like what I thought they were saying better than what they are actually saying. But I love words and their power when used properly. Songs can put words together that I sometimes can't, especially when I'm deep in my feelings.

Music unites us in a way that not much else can. When you are with someone, listening to a song you both like, your differences cease to matter. I've listened to songs before that made me realize I'm not crazy for thinking or feeling like I do. Don't ever feel crazy for thinking or feeling the way you do. All thoughts and feelings are valid, meaningful, and valuable.

Music is something that has been around since the beginning of time. God created music, and he knew that it was good!

While researching for this book, I came across a song that I'd never heard but wanted to listen to again and again. It's called "Gypsy Soul" by Rachel Morgan Perry. I couldn't find the lyrics online, so I sent a Facebook message to the artist and was pleased when she replied. Here are the lyrics:

Ruby-red lips and light blonde hair
But there's a whole lot more than that
Contagious smile that's so sincere
Makes you wanna live like that
But people are mean, and told her things
That aren't true
So she traded in her love for life leaving her
Empty and bruised
And there she goes
Living like a gypsy soul
Lost and out of use
Thinking that everything that she's done
She can't undo
Well, angel, don't you know there's a whole lot more

A whole lot more to you
Oh, baby blue eyes
Go back to you
November leaves, they start to fall
And while they fall, she does too
Perfect like an antique doll
She wants to feel beautiful and new
This girl once full of life was robbed of everything she knew
The world, it pulled and tugged 'til she was left
Jaded and confused
And there she goes
Living like a gypsy soul
Lost and out of use
Thinking that everything that she's done
She can't undo
Well, angel, don't you know there's a whole lot more
A whole lot more to you
Oh, baby blue eyes
Go back to you
Hope it shines down on you and you don't even know
It's mostly broken hearts
That change the world[6]

I love this song. It puts words to my current season of life. The artist wrote this song in 2013, and without knowing me, she wrote a song for my life nine years before I would discover the song and live it. The lyrics probably have a different meaning for her life, but isn't it incredibly beautiful how music works? We all interpret it differently and let it speak to us in different ways. The only piece

---

6 Rachel Morgan Perry, "Gypsy Soul," YouTube video, 3:59, May 2, 2013, https://www.youtube.com/watch?v=317zfzVrP28. Lyrics used with permission by Rachel Morgan Perry.

I don't identify with in this song is the ruby-red lips, but maybe it's a sign that I should try that out! I'm fairly certain she is referring to living like a gypsy soul because of her situation, and a gypsy soul is not who she really is. But in my case, my situation has caused me to discover my gypsy soul and how much more there is to me.

I have tried to keep myself in this cage of what I think I should be or am expected to be. I traded who I am for the status quo. I've made mistakes and felt trapped by those mistakes, but I made those mistakes because I wasn't living as my authentic self. I can relate to this song even down to the specifics of this stanza:

November leaves, they start to fall
And while they fall, she does too
Perfect like an antique doll
She wants to feel beautiful and new

It was in November that I fell to the bottom of the pit, trying to be a good enough wife in my new marriage to an abusive man. But I couldn't live—truly live—in that environment. I was not encouraged to live authentically, but to live for how others perceived us. I was so beaten down emotionally and mentally. Then I decided to choose myself, and I left.

I wanted to be beautiful and new, authentic. And I accomplished that! I created a new life for myself, leaving the past where it was, and I feel beautiful! I love my life and myself! I'm back to me, and so full of life again.

I wouldn't be where I am now without all my good and bad experiences. I never lost hope. My heart has been broken over and over again throughout my life, but I think Rachel, the writer of the lyrics, is spot-on when she says, "It's mostly broken hearts that change the world."

Thank you, Rachel, for writing this song, recording it, and responding to my request for the lyrics. I hope my story can inspire you the way you inspired me.

I love nature and art. I am imaginative and creative. Music runs through my veins!

8

"You have to leave the city
of your comfort and
go into the wilderness
of your intuition."
—Alan Alda

You let your emotions guide you. You are empathetic. You trust your intuition.

I have always felt things deeply. Childhood trauma flooded my little mind with feelings I didn't know what to do with. I didn't know how to label these feelings individually or collectively, and even if I could have, there was no one to tell. I didn't have a way to escape the confusion other than disassociating from the situation. When you disassociate from something, you are physically there, but you are not there either; you just float away. I learned quickly how to disconnect from my mind and body, but dissociation is only a temporary coping mechanism. Eventually, at least in my case, I was going to have to feel all the feelings.

My feelings started to overflow in the form of daily uncontrollable tears at the most inconvenient times, starting in sixth grade. I would be in math class, thinking about dividing 254 by 12, and my paper would become dotted with tears. I battled to hold them back, and if anyone noticed, I would act like I had something in my eye. I was scared. What if they figured out my secret? I had so much shame and couldn't stop the tears from pouring out. I would go to the bathroom, but couldn't be gone for too long, or someone would wonder. I felt so weak and powerless, so embarrassed. I had no control over this, and the harder I tried to shore things up, the stronger the tears would fight to seep out. At a time when I should have been worrying about getting good grades, whether my hair looked just right, or if I would win the next four-square game at recess, I was tormented with emotions getting in my face, demanding to be seen and felt. I battled with this for months, but ultimately got better at hiding what was happening.

Today, I don't make my emotions have to fight their way out. However, they still can be confusing and hard to name. Sometimes I have to look at a list of feelings to help me narrow down how I feel or to get more specific about a feeling. My feelings are complex, they can change quickly, and sometimes they even contradict themselves. I can be very fragile, but appear strong at the same time. People say I am so strong for surviving what I endured during my childhood. Not true. I was a child. I didn't need to be stronger; I needed to be safe. Being strong had nothing to do with it. No, my trauma just made me traumatized. I lived in survival mode. I did what I had to do and became who I had to become to survive.

Trauma and pain do not make you stronger; they make you softer and more compassionate. It makes you empathetic to others and their struggles. Strength doesn't define survivors, but softness and kindness do. It makes me unafraid to live in confusing or unpredictable environments, and I'm comfortable with taking risks. Survival mode is familiar to me, almost normal. There is no "before trauma" as a childhood abuse survivor. I have no reference point to who I was before; this is who I am and have always been.

When you feel emotions at such a complex level and struggle to describe them, others might assume you are being thoughtless, when in fact, you are deep in your thoughts; you are just struggling to express them properly, adequately, or truthfully. You feel not only your own emotions, but those of the people close to you, making you empathetic to other people's situations, even if it's outside something you have experienced. The ability to put yourself in someone else's shoes comes easily. Being an emotional and empathetic person can make it easier for you to get hurt, but it also allows you to experience life to its fullest.

⌁

Intuition is often referred to as a woman's sixth sense. It's not gender-specific though. I know I am an intuitive person; I notice things, I am an observer, and I pay attention to details. But somewhere along the way, I learned or was taught to distrust my intuition and ignore it instead.

After being divorced for a year, I met someone who seemed to be a quality person, but in time, what appeared to be good was very, very dysfunctional. I quickly began losing my identity and all I had worked hard to become. I was not experienced in dating and was being taken advantage of and promised things my logical mind knew would never happen. I felt like I was watching my life play out before my eyes, with no control over it.

I didn't realize it, but I had disassociated myself from this situation. I knew this wasn't what I wanted and that this wasn't God's plan for me. I felt trapped and controlled. I could see everything that was happening from two perspectives: My logical perspective (intuition) told me this relationship was wrong and unhealthy for me. My emotional perspective then explained away unexplainable behavior. Had I listened to my intuition from the beginning, I would have saved myself a lot of money and grief.

I saw so much good in this man that he couldn't see. Maybe I was there to help him find it. On the other hand, maybe he was never willing to look for it. I've learned over the years that I become attracted and attached to what could be. This prevents me from seeing and accepting who someone has proven themselves to be. I can find value and meaning in any hint of potential, even when I know it's not good for my own mental health. I was chasing after every scrap of love and affection thrown at me. I continued this pattern in future relationships until I finally learned my lesson— the hard way.

Another stumbling block when it comes to emotions and intuition that has carried into my adult life is thinking abuse and love can coexist. They cannot. Based on this notion, I have made unbelievably bad decisions in my romantic life. I can easily rationalize being hurt by someone and insist it is okay because they love me. It took me a couple different relationship experiences and fifteen years to realize what I was doing and why it wasn't working.

Learning to trust my intuition is hard. Accepting that my

emotions are valid is tough. Our intuition and emotions are gifts; they are there to protect us.

I believe everything happens for a reason. People change so we can learn to let go. Things go wrong so we can appreciate things going right. We believe lies so eventually we can learn to trust ourselves. Sometimes good things fall apart so better things can come together.

I have caused myself so much heartbreak over and over and over again. I've still got work to do in this area and will learn to recognize my intuition as an integral part of my being and start trusting it.

Be yourself. Let people see the real, imperfect, flawed, quirky, weird, beautiful, and magical person you are. I don't know who I would be without my emotions. I saw a quote recently from Karen Clark about people who lead with their emotions: "The thing about your emotions is that they aren't tamed; it's easy for you to get very happy or very sad."[7]

I love the idea of emotions being untamed! Our emotions are fluid, living, and ever-changing, and if you want to live an authentic life, they must never be tamed! It becomes a balancing act, trying to find a happy medium. One moment I can be happy, sociable, and present, and the next I can be detached and distant and need to be alone.

If you didn't know me, you might think I'm flighty or can't make up my mind, but it's the paradox I live in. I'm easily bored and will play the devil's advocate when I make decisions so I can refine my thinking and make sure I have looked at a situation from

7 Karen Clark, "11 Signs You Are a Woman with a Gypsy Soul," Think Aloud, last modified January 10, 2022, https:// thinkaloud.net/11-signs-you-are-a-woman-with-a-gypsy-soul/.

every possible vantage point. Then I still struggle to decide. The only quick decisions I make are those where you tell me I must do something or I can't do something. I will undoubtedly do whatever you say I can't, or won't do something you set as a condition!

I am an emotional, empathetic person who is learning to trust my intuition.

9

"The cave you fear to enter
holds the treasure you seek."
–Joseph Campbell

**You believe in magic
and miracles.
You are optimistic and
know something good
is always around
the corner.**

One Christmas Eve, we headed to church and then to my grand-parents' for the evening. I was so excited for Santa to come! I was young enough to still believe, but I was starting to wonder. I re-member being especially excited because I wanted nothing more than a Cabbage Patch Kid doll that year! We came home late that night from my grandparents'; it was after midnight. We walked into the house, and Santa had come while we were gone! I couldn't believe it. *And* he brought me a Cabbage Patch Kid!

I was as curious about how Santa had known we were gone as I was excited about my new doll. Years later, I asked my mom how that happened or who she had come over to our house as Santa. She was surprised I hadn't figured out that she had "forgotten" something in the house and had to go back in once we were all in the car. It was the most magical Christmas I remember as a kid.

—————

I am a Jesus lover and a miracle believer! I receive God's grace every single day of my life. He has paid my bills when I knew there was no other way, kept me safe when I was in imminent danger, and not only given me courage when I was scared to death, but walked through it right next to me the whole time. He is my savior, my protector, my healer, my father, my peace, the one who fulfills my heart's desire. He is walking on this walk of self-discovery with me right now as he reveals the parts of myself I have been trying to stuff down. His light is shining on and through me!

We all know those princess stories that end with the knight in shining armor rescuing the damsel in distress. I am a princess, and Jesus is my knight in shining armor—no joke. Although I sometimes forget, he reminds me, and I rest in his gentle arms and remember that he is the only one who can meet my needs and make me totally free.

—————

I was twenty years old and pregnant with my first child when my dad died. My dad had cancer in the lining of his heart, which is exceedingly rare. He had battled through rounds of chemo and radiation, but the inevitable was near. The night he died was unremarkable in comparison to the previous several nights. Dad had been in somewhat of a coma for about a week. The hospice nurse told us this is very natural toward the end. We noticed his breathing was labored and faster. I told my mom we needed to call the nurse because something was wrong. Mom said, "No, we can't call her every time something changes." His breathing continued like this until late into the night; we knew something was happening. He seemed to be distressed. After more than a week of not opening his eyes or making any movements or noise, he was trying to move his head and was moaning. We decided it was time to call the nurse. She was with another patient but came as soon as she could. We also called my grandparents, aunt, and uncle. My brother and one aunt were already there.

We sat around Dad's bed, Mom on one side, me on the other, and held his hands. We breathed as fast as he did and watched his chest rise and fall. Each breath seemed to get faster and more labored. He moaned and turned his head as he forced his eyes open. He struggled each time, but continued doing this. It was as if he were looking at each of us, one by one, saying goodbye. We all breathed in and out just as Dad did. Then as suddenly as his breathing had increased, it started to get slower. We all silently wondered, *Is this the end?* Slower, slower, in, out, in, out, in ... silence. No one in the room was breathing. My world had stopped, but the room was spinning. My daddy was gone.

As I sat there, breathless, with his hand in mine, a calm and gentle peace came over me. It was a strange, unfamiliar feeling. I felt comfort knowing my dad was no longer suffering or hurting. I felt as if we were in a different part of the room, far away from everyone else, just me and my dad. In the background, I could hear loud sobs and cries of mourning, but my mind, heart, and soul were still. This mysterious comfort that draped over me only lasted a few minutes, then it was gone. I am so thankful for that moment. It was magical. It was a miracle.

When I visited any beach on my 2016 road trip, I always looked for fun shells, sea glass, and sand dollars. I wanted to find some sand dollars to take home. Being from Nebraska, I was inexperienced with the ocean. I learned a couple things pretty quickly. First, the ocean is extremely hard to stand still in, and it really doesn't care if you only want to get wet from the waist down. Second, although I never needed to have this fact proven to me, I unwillingly confirmed what I already knew: yep, the water is salty! The ocean has a mind of its own.

While I was at Ocracoke Island on the outer banks of North Carolina, I talked with a couple of local girls at a restaurant. After talking with them, I was fairly sure I was going to be able to find sand dollars there at low tide. The girls taught me about high and low tide, what that meant, and how the timing changed each day according to the moon. During my time there, low tide was going to be at 3:58 a.m. I didn't care; I wanted to find a sand dollar!

I set my alarm for 3:45 a.m., and with a flashlight and pail in tow, I headed to the beach. It was eerie walking out there in complete darkness, alone except for the moonlight. Because it was low tide, I was now crossing a much larger beach than earlier in the day. I walked along the water, and it wasn't long before I found a sand dollar, a small one, about the size of a quarter. I don't know how I found it, because I was looking for something much larger! I had to search for the next two, but was so happy to have found three.

I did find a larger one, but when I put him in my basket, he moved. The girls I met at the restaurant told me that if you put them in your hand and they turn green, they are still alive. I didn't think he was alive, but he obviously was. I looked at him for a bit and reluctantly threw him back. The three smaller ones were a brown, purply color. The white ones you see in stores are bleached.

After about an hour and a half, I decided it was time to go back to bed.

I knew there would come a time when I would be ready to spread my wings and fly away from the comfort, connection, and familiarity of Nebraska. I felt the need to discover new territory. I made it a goal to move during the summer of 2020 to a tiny house community in North Carolina. My daughter would be halfway through college, and I felt it would be viewed as more socially acceptable for me to move halfway across the country at that point.

To my surprise, my daughter gave me her blessing to go in the fall of 2018, so my plans moved forward, and I moved to North Carolina into the tiny house community where I was called to be. When you move to a town with no family or friends, you see how strong you are. The risk you're afraid to take could change your life; it did mine.

I used to be an extreme dog hater, no exaggeration. I had a very strong dislike for dogs. My son called one day while he was living with roommates in a house that didn't allow pets. He said he'd found a dog and was going to keep him. My first response was that finding a dog didn't work that way, but we went through all the proper channels to report him lost and allow him to be claimed. After thirty days, if no one claimed him, my son could keep him. Until that time, we were considered to be fostering the dog.

Since my son couldn't have pets at his house, he said he was bringing him to mine. I told him, "No, no, no! You are not bringing a dog to my house!" After going round and round, I agreed to keep the varmint in my basement bathroom, making it clear I would have nothing to do with it. My son would have to come to feed it and let it out. I didn't want to see, smell, or hear anything! Well, Carlos—the abandoned Shih Tzu-poodle with an active tail that made his whole hind end move from side to side—wiggled his way right into my heart—and my bed!

Never having had a dog before and not being a dog lover, I thought it would only slobber on me and look at me like a dumb dog if I ever told it to do anything. I know—pure ignorance! I quickly fell in love with Carlos and his big personality. I looked forward to coming home and being greeted by that waggling butt, so happy to see me.

After Carlos had been at my house for a few months, on Easter morning, I came home from church. My daughter was not home, and my son had come to claim his dog while I was gone. He was now living in a place where he could keep Carlos. The joy I had coming home from the Easter service was gone when I opened the door, noticing no waggling butt happy to see me! I resolved at that moment to get a dog, a waggling butt of my own who would be happy to see me when I came home!

I now have a little dog named Henry. He is a Havapoo—part Havanese, part poodle. He is seven pounds of pure spoiled fur! He is the first dog I've ever had, and he'll be the last; there is just no replacing him.

⁓

Moving to North Carolina felt like a dream come true. But after being there for just over a month, it wasn't feeling like the dream I had imagined. Frustrations, tears, lonely days and nights, and thoughts of *What in the hell did I just do?* raced through my head. As exciting and brave as it may have been, many fears, anxieties, and uncertainty came along with pursuing my dreams.

When planning for this move, I was fully aware of what I was getting into. I was moving to a new state after living in one state for my entire life. I didn't know anyone where I moved to, I didn't know how to get around this new area (thank God for Google Maps!), and I missed my kids and family like crazy. I knew I'd meet new people and figure out how to get around, and I knew I'd never take seeing my kids and family for granted.

I was supposed to be moved and settling into my new home by October 1. The sale of my Nebraska house was quick and closed on September 13. I then made my way to North Carolina to the rental where I'd be staying for a couple of weeks before my house was ready. I had loaded all the items I thought I would need for the interim in the front passenger seat so they would be easy to access. Everything else would stay in the car until I was ready to unload it into my new house.

My move-in date was pushed back to November 1, which was disappointing, but I was flexible. After being in this new place for a month, still waiting to move into my house, I had many unanticipated feelings and experiences while trying to acclimate myself to a place I now called home.

I've never been one to have a lot of close friends or friends that I would hang out with routinely, so I never imagined that moving to a place where I didn't know anyone would be an issue. It turns out that even though they weren't close friends, I still had a tribe who were "my people" back in Nebraska! I would see "my people" at church, familiar faces at the grocery store, my neighbors, and even local news anchors. My parents would pop in, and of course, the kids would be around now and again. My tribe, my people, were around every day, whether I knew them by name or not. They were familiar.

In this new place, I had no people. I had nothing familiar. The streets I drove were all new, and there were no familiar landmarks. I'd go to the grocery store, or any store for that matter, and nothing was familiar—not the people, not the layout of the store, or even the location of the toilet paper. It was an exciting adventure at first, but it started to wear on my soul that I was alone. No one knew if I belonged there or not; maybe they just hadn't noticed me before.

It took me some time before I realized the miracle Henry was, the purpose he served, and why God changed my heart about dogs. Nothing felt normal or gave me the comfort of home except Henry. Henry was part of God's plan from the very beginning. I needed the time with him in Nebraska to get to know him, bond with him, and let him weave himself into my heart. Henry was God's gift to me and my saving grace the first few months after moving to a new, unfamiliar place. God knew, long before I did, what I would need, where my path would lead, and the struggles I would face. Henry was my miracle. He is one miracle of many that God has performed in my life. I know miracles will continue to grace my life and will surprise me each and every time they happen.

There was so much to do within a short distance of where I lived, so I figured there wouldn't be a chance for me to get bored. I liked spending time alone. I was social, but only when I wanted to be and when I didn't feel awkward because I was a stranger. I wanted to go out and explore the different towns near me, maybe go on a hike, drive through the mountains, and get lost in my new world. But I didn't want to leave Henry because I knew he would just sit staring out the window, waiting for me to return. It would make me feel so guilty. Before I moved, he had a dog door, so I never had to worry about letting him out. Never having had that worry before, I didn't know how long he could be left before needing out; plus, he was in a new place too. I didn't want him to worry about whether I was coming back or not. I could take him with me, but the car was a place he really didn't care to be after the two-and-a-half-day trip, and the car was still full since I hadn't unpacked.

For some unknown reason, I didn't think I would need tennis shoes until after I unpacked. I thought I would need socks—two pairs—but not tennis shoes! Of course, I knew right where they were in my car, but getting them would be like opening one of those round cans of biscuits and then trying to put all the biscuits back in. I love to do puzzles, so I thought I would buy a puzzle, and that would keep me busy. Then I realized there wasn't even a table in the house I was staying in, and if I put it together on the floor, Henry would think the pieces were snacks. Henry loved that we filled so much of our time on walks, and soon all these struggles would be distant memories once we enjoyed settling into our new house.

I was missing my church, my kids, my family, my friends,

fellow Husker fans, and some things packed away in the car that made life more convenient or entertaining. I expected to miss those things, but there were so many feelings I didn't expect. Don't get the wrong idea; I had no regrets, just unexpected trials to overcome. I genuinely loved it there, despite the challenges. I knew I was exactly where I was supposed to be. I knew things would get easier and better. I had already met some wonderful people who lived in my community and would in time become friends. After all, the community was what drew me to this place (and wanting to live in a tiny house)!

I never really understood why people would say I was brave for doing what I was doing. Now I get it. My bravery, faith, and strength were indeed tested during those first months.

We all need a little refining now and again so we can shine brighter where we are planted.

———

Most people have heard of the Japanese word *kintsugi*, or at least heard of the concept. It is the art of putting broken pottery pieces back together with gold. What a wonderful and powerful way to treat something that is broken! I like to think of myself as a piece of broken pottery. Being broken and healing is part of our journey and should not be hidden or removed from our stories. I know there is a purpose for my brokenness. Someone needs to hear my story. I have heard hundreds of broken stories over my lifetime that have influenced me, helped me heal, and given me the courage to accept my brokenness and let it show.

The hurt and pain I have encountered in my life will not be in vain. Escaping my childhood trauma was nothing short of a miracle, and it strengthened my faith in a God who never abandoned me, even through my darkest times. I am proud of my flawed and imperfect self. Something good will come out of my history. God makes beauty out of ashes. Like the song "Beautiful Things" by Michael Gungor says:

You make beautiful things
You make beautiful things out of the dust
You make beautiful things
You make beautiful things out of us [8]

Take a minute to listen to the song now, or whenever you need some encouragement or inspiration.

Imagine a world where people are not seen as damaged or broken, but their traumas and hurts are highlighted as events in their lives. Instead of exploiting those events, we celebrate and focus on them as something made beautiful because of their brokenness. We are all imperfect humans, so why keep trying to appear as though we are not? When we choose to heal or make something beautiful out of our imperfect lives, it's like *kintsugi* for our soul, a way to accept that things happen and things change, and an assurance that this is a fact of human life.

I believe in magic and miracles. I am optimistic and know something good is always around the corner!

8 Michael Gungor and Lisa Gungor, "Beautiful Things," Copyright © 2009 worshiptogether.com Songs (ASCAP) (adm.at CapitolCMGPublishing.com) All rights reserved. Used by permission.

10

"I won't tell you that the world matters nothing, or the world's voice, or the voice of society. They matter a good deal. They matter far too much. But there are moments when one has to choose between living one's own life, fully, entirely, completely—or dragging out some false, shallow, degrading existence that the world in its hypocrisy demands. You have that moment now. Choose!"

−Oscar Wilde

You dance to the beat of your own drum and live an unconventional lifestyle. You're constantly looking for something new and exciting.

When planning my 2016 road trip, I would get mixed reactions from people. Some would comment about how awesome it would be, how brave they thought I was, and how crazy they thought I was. Some worried about my safety, and more wondered how I could take off and roam without much of a plan other than a rough idea of the route I would take.

I also had kids and a house—responsibilities that you just don't abandon. My daughter was sixteen and still in high school, and I was leaving in the middle of the school year. People asked me what she would do (she was living with me full-time at this point) and what she thought about all this. I'm sure she thought I was crazy too, but she was used to her mom being unpredictable by this point. She had a car and a driver's license and was a responsible sixteen-year-old. She stayed with my parents mostly, and sometimes with her dad. Even if she thought it was crazy, she was sixteen, so she probably thought it would be a nice break from her mom! She was and is very close to her granny and papa and even had her own room at their house.

Having worked seasonally in the tax industry for years, I've become a pro at stretching the income I make in four months to cover my expenses for the entire year. This feat alone has puzzled people for a long time, especially during the off-season when I wasn't working. I knew people were curious about how I lived. I'm sure they thought that a single mother working only four months a year must either be on welfare or secretly wealthy, but I was neither. I worked a lot of hours during tax season, and some years I did work more than just during tax season. I would teach tax classes part-time in the evenings from September to December. Other years, I'd get a part-time job during the off-season. It just depended on my financial needs for the year.

My expenses were predictable, so I could easily determine what I needed to earn for the year to cover my expenses. Anything above and beyond that was optional. I'm sure some of you are now thinking, *She is crazy*, when I used the word "optional." Who refers to income as optional? That unconventional concept alone is something that only someone who dances to the beat of their own drum would say. But to me, you work to live, not live to work.

I wanted freedom. If there were things I wanted to do or places I wanted to go, I made sure I earned enough to do those things. I got clear on what I really needed and wanted in my life. I didn't want things that were unnecessary, weighed me down, or stressed me out. This realization didn't happen overnight, and this change of mindset was not like a light switch. Thoughts tumbled around in my head like puzzle pieces. Gradually, I would fit some pieces together and occasionally get glimpses of what the image of this puzzle might look like. I liked it! Unconventional, yes, but I was stress-free, well-rested, able to have time for the things I wanted to have time for, content, and free.

Today, I would say I am a liberal minimalist. Some minimalists are hardcore, only the bare necessities, but I am not quite that extreme. I am too big a fan of creature comforts!

Families and parenting today look quite different than they did two generations ago, when I was raised. It was just starting to become acceptable to have two working parents. Divorce existed, but was not prevalent. Kids were told not to speak until spoken to, and they followed that instruction. For the most part, spanking was still accepted and effective, respect for elders was nonnegotiable, and families usually ate dinner together. Many of us grew up in two-income families, so we became latchkey kids, fending for ourselves after school. Talking back to our parents was not tolerated.

By the time my kids were born, families and parenting had changed, as it does with every generation. Divorce was a bit more prevalent, but still not overly common. Children were encouraged to speak for themselves. Discipline changed from spanking to time-out, and nontraditional families were becoming more commonplace. Single moms, unmarried parents, or grandparents raising grandkids were starting to emerge. It seemed like everyone, at least in Nebraska, knew of someone who would fit in this category.

In my case, divorcing at age twenty-nine, with the kids going back and forth between the parents each week, was unconventional. But I was okay with being different. I have always felt a little different than my peers anyhow, so this was just another difference to add to the list. My ex-husband and I had only grown apart; we didn't necessarily hate each other, so we did a decent job of helping our kids adjust to their new way of life.

Leaving my daughter with her grandparents to go on a road trip during the school year was unconventional too, but it wasn't crazy. That road trip was life-changing for me and has become part of the legacy I will leave. I broke out of the box. I started dancing to the beat of my own drum. I showed my kids it's okay to go after your dreams, to do things differently, to be scared and do it anyway, to not wait for someday to do something, that the world is so much bigger than the city or town you grow up in, and that it's okay to do things on your own, even if everyone else thinks you're crazy.

Experiences are better than things. You are braver than you think you are. It's okay to get out of your comfort zone. And you never know until you try!

Since that road trip, I am always looking for something new and exciting. I learned the world is much bigger than the bubble

I lived in. I am more capable than I imagined. I thrived in an ever-changing environment. I didn't need permission or another person to start living my life. I was a dandelion in the wind, ready to be carried to wherever the wind blew me. I could hear the beat of my own drum and I started dancing to it.

I can handle roughing it when it comes to accommodations. I don't require much, and I'm not uncomfortable living without some of the common modern conveniences. I discovered something that I do require, however: I cannot sleep in hot, humid weather without a fan, where you wake up sweating.

Recently, a friend and I traveled to Tulum, Mexico. Tulum is a beautiful tropical jungle city. We stayed at a solar-powered Airbnb. A generator would run air conditioning from 8:00 p.m. until 9:00 a.m. each day. Assuming we would be out most days and back after the air conditioning was running, it seemed like a reasonable setup. Or it might have been—if the air conditioner had worked consistently. Sometimes it would run well for about three hours and then be done blowing any cool air, and it became a regular fan on the wall blowing hot air. One night it worked for about three hours and then completely shut off. We found out later that the generator had run out of fuel. After four nights of lying in our beds wearing as little clothes as possible, trying and failing to sleep, constantly being sweaty and sticky, with sunburnt skin, and watching lizards climb up the walls, we couldn't take any more.

Jesus is always with me and makes his presence most known when I am traveling. Even Jesus was hot at this point! We decided for our last night to get a room at a hotel in town, a trusted chain with all-day air conditioning that worked, and Jesus led us right to Enrique! After we arrived at the hotel, we met Enrique, who checked us in. We saw his halo start to glow when he told us they had a room ready so that we could check in early, and he even surprised us with an upgraded room. We felt like we had just entered heaven! We walked into our cool, air-conditioned room, took quick showers to rinse the sticky sweat off, and immediately lay in our beds for a siesta!

———

Trying something I have never tried before is usually fun. I will try most anything at least once. I visited Bathhouse Row when I was in Hot Springs, Arkansas. That was quite the experience. I was transported back to the early 1900s, when these facilities were popular. I went to the Buckstaff Bath House, which originally opened in 1912 and has not been modernized much. This made it an even more historic experience.

I was escorted to the second floor, the ladies' floor, where a bath attendant took me to a locker room. She told me to call for her when I was undressed, and she would drape me. It's basically a toga, but I had never been "draped" before. I was then led to the bath, equipped with a contraption that looked like a small antique trolling motor. The attendant helped me into the tub. When I arrived, I had been given a loofah; she took it and scrubbed my back, feet, and legs. She added more water until the bath was at 104 degrees and placed a board behind my back that I could lean against. I was comfortable and given two small cups of warm water to drink. The attendant turned on the trolling motor, and I was now sitting in a whirlpool. Twenty blissful minutes passed, then she came to help me out of the tub and draped me in another sheet. I was then taken to a table where I got hot packs—and I mean *hot*! I laid on these hot packs, which were essentially really hot wet towels. Then they placed more hot packs on my legs, wrapped my head in a cold towel, and gave me ice cubes to put in my mouth.

The next step was to visit the steam chamber. This was a space-age-looking box that I'm sure made me look like the Tin Man's cousin. It was a metal box that closed around me with flaps over my shoulders, so only my head was sticking out—very 1912-ish!

Up next was a sitz bath. I had never had a sitz bath, not even a modern-day one. It's an actual porcelain bath made to sit in. I had seen them before in tours of houses from that time period, but hadn't realized that's what they were. It was amazingly comfortable, just extremely hot.

After the sitz bath was the needle shower. I wasn't sure about this part from the name, but it was just a full-body shower with water from pipes spraying at you from all directions. I was so delighted with the whole experience. I would probably do it again if given the opportunity; it was a new and exciting experience.

⁓

In 2020, when COVID-19 started, I found myself calling off an engagement and needing to find a new place to live. I had already sold my tiny house at this point. The world was panicking, not knowing what COVID would bring, so it was difficult to find anywhere to rent temporarily until I made a plan. I ended up buying a thirty-three-foot motorhome and living in it. There are a lot of full-time RVers, and I had enjoyed my road trip, so this seemed like a wise choice at the time. It was—for the most part.

I lived in my motorhome for ten months. I had considered a camper van because I wanted to be mobile, like I was on my road trip, but I ultimately decided the additional space was the better option since I would be working and living in it. I had Henry to consider now too; I didn't have him during my road trip. Reflecting back on that decision now, I wish I would have chosen a camper van for easier mobility. If I had gone with a camper van, I think the following couple years of my life would have taken a different course than it did.

I found a campground in upstate South Carolina. I didn't have time to research and figure out my preferences. I just had to get moved in and set up, as I was in the middle of tax season. This RV living had a steep learning curve since I had never done it or even considered it before. Fortunately, my parents had an RV and traveled quite a bit, so they were able to help me learn the ropes.

Coming from Tornado Alley in Nebraska, I never expected that tornados would be something I'd experience in South Carolina! Still, during the two months I was at this campground, there were four tornado warnings. I stayed in my motorhome each time and said I would never do that again. I just didn't know what else to do or where to go.

After two months, I wanted to go somewhere else. The campground felt like an asphalt parking lot because it was new and had very few trees. If you have lived in South Carolina before, you know how hot it can get, and even more so when you are parked on new asphalt. But I had immense anxiety about changing locations. I had this big motorhome to drive that I'd only driven twice, for a short distance, and I would have to tow my car behind. But my parents are angels and drove from Nebraska to South Carolina to caravan with me to my new location.

I could go anywhere in the US I wanted. I was missing the mountains of Western North Carolina, so I chose to go to the

Ozark Mountains. I had been there as a kid and assumed it would be similar to the mountains of Western North Carolina. So, I moved to Eureka Springs, Arkansas. It was beautiful there. But it was not like the mountains I was missing—at least, not weather-wise. It was hot and humid, and I wanted the cool mountain temperatures I had become accustomed to.

After caravaning with my parents, I was more comfortable driving the motorhome and towing my car. Still, it was not necessarily an easy process to unhook and prepare everything inside and out for traveling, especially for my inexperienced self. I waited it out, telling myself I needed to just hold still for a while. I hadn't met anyone there because I was in a tourist location. Everyone I'd met so far was just visiting or didn't actually live in Eureka Springs. I felt so alone during this time, but was forcing myself to stay.

I joined many Facebook groups related to full-time RVing, and an ad came up for Amazon CamperForce. It was essentially a temporary job for RVers. You would work at an Amazon fulfillment center for three to four months during the holiday season. There were several locations to choose from, you made good money, and Amazon would pay for your campsite for the duration of time you worked, which made it even more of a lucrative opportunity; campgrounds are usually over five hundred dollars a month for a space. I filled out the application, which included some basic testing, and was hired that day. I chose the location in Lebanon, Tennessee, just outside of Nashville. It was the end of July, and I decided to start in September instead of October, so I started preparing to go to Nebraska for the month of August and then arrive in Tennessee at the beginning of September.

You choose your location with CamperForce and what campground you want from their approved list, but you do not get to choose the shift or schedule you work or what job you do. You are assigned a ten-hour day or night shift for four days a week with a job in picking, receiving, stowing, or shipping. I was assigned the donut night shift in receiving. The donut shift meant I would work Monday, Tuesday, Thursday, and Friday. No one seemed to want that shift because they wanted three days off in a row, but for me, I loved having at least one day off every two days. That also helped me adjust to working overnight from 6:00 p.m. to 4:30 a.m.! It took a bit to adjust, but once I did, it was okay. I wouldn't normally choose to work overnight, ever! But my job in receiving was something I enjoyed. It was a physical job, which I liked. The hard part was standing on my feet for that long, but as with anything, I adjusted.

There were two lines of conveyor belts. One was the large line, the other the small line. If an item was large or weighed more than fifty pounds, it went to the large line. As items came down the line, you would take them off, receive the item into the computer, and place it in a cart or cage. When your cart or cage was full, it would be taken to the next stage, where stowers would put the items in the correct aisle. I was surprised at how much I enjoyed the job. Everything is tracked, from the number of items you receive each hour to the accuracy of items in each of your carts or cages to the seconds it takes you between receiving items. I had high numbers, so I was eventually moved to the Hazmat Department, receiving everything from nail polish to perfume. Usually, but not always, these were smaller items placed into stackable bins on pallets instead of carts or cages. Hazmat was even more enjoyable to me. I would try to challenge myself with the number of items I could receive in an hour. One day I ranked first out of 479 receivers! I received 11,702 items during a single shift. Now, mind you, I was probably receiving nail polish or something else small at the time that came in boxes of twenty or more, so I was just opening and dumping.

By the time December came, I was ready for a break. We had been working overtime, and the nights were wearing on me. During the time I was in Tennessee, I decided I wanted to move back to the North Carolina mountains, a bit farther west than where I had been originally. I was over living in an RV. If I had initially gone with a camper van and felt more mobile, I would probably still be traveling around today.

I had decided early on in my pregnancy with my son that I did not want to have an epidural. I didn't want any drugs; I wanted to deliver him naturally. My justification was that God had made my body to do this, so I was going to do it. After twenty-seven and a half hours of natural labor, he was born. I would not recommend natural labor. Indeed, God made my body capable of doing this— but he also made drugs!

My son can be a little unconventional and has always danced to the beat of his own drum too. When he was in high school, his first-period teacher allowed the students to bring breakfast to class and even encouraged it. Instead of bringing cereal or a breakfast bar like the other students, my son thought outside the box and was a bit of a jokester. He showed up to class with pancake mix and a waffle maker. Not quite what the teacher had in mind, but I love how he thinks!

I dance to the beat of my own drum and live an unconventional lifestyle. I am constantly looking for something new and exciting.

11

"Travel is at its most rewarding
when it ceases to be about your reaching
a destination and becomes indistinguishable
from living your life."
—Paul Theroux

You are a free-spirited, adventurous wanderer who loves your freedom.

When I grew up in a small Nebraska town, kids spent their days outside and used their imagination to create their own fun. We would ride our bikes around and find something interesting to do. As a friend and I were riding around town, we came across a wooded area by the legion hall. Not thick woods, but it was right off the road and looked like a good place to explore. We laid our bikes on the side of the road and went in.

Leaves and fallen branches covered the ground. We started

clearing a small space and were going to make a clubhouse! Not a physical structure, but a place only we knew about and could go hide out. We moved the fallen branches to create the perimeter and shifted large stumps and branches into a seating area. It was so exciting; we would make it just how we liked it and hoped no one would come along to disturb it. I don't remember beyond that first day when we prepared the space. Maybe we returned a time or two, but certainly we were on to different places and greater adventures.

Eventually, we left our bikes behind and started to drive— something you learned early in rural areas. My area to explore grew larger. I got my learner's permit at thirteen and my school permit at fourteen. I was driving myself and my best friend to school each day when I was just fourteen! When my kids were fourteen, there was no way I would have trusted them to drive, even in a rural area, much less on the snow-and-ice-covered highway we drove to get to school.

I had always been more mature and responsible than others my age. We would sometimes go the back way home, taking the gravel roads just for a change of scenery. We would also spend many evenings just driving around. My best friend would call, or I would call her when we were ready to go. It was a nightly activity and something I think a lot of Midwestern kids grew up doing. We would cruise O Street in Lincoln on the weekends, and during the week, my friend and I would cruise around our small town. Nowhere in particular to go; we just drove and talked. I started smoking cigarettes when I was thirteen, thanks to my older brother's girlfriend. My best friend started smoking a few years later, so this was the ideal time to smoke; it became more of the reason our drives were a nightly activity.

We felt free from parents and homework to wander aimlessly along the dark streets or down the country roads. It was something we both looked forward to, and I think the freedom of those drives stuck with me. I wanted to be somewhere other than where I was, hoping I would find something new and exciting along the way, but we knew those roads like the backs of our hands, so that didn't happen much. Still, it was a way for me to let my spirit be free.

I would not have described myself as a free spirit or adventurous until later in adulthood. I married three weeks after I turned nineteen and had my first child at twenty-one and my second at twenty-four. I would not recommend this—not the children part, but the married-at-nineteen part!

By the time I was in my late twenties, I was pretty miserable. My husband and I no longer had a connection beyond our kids' lives. We had no common interests or goals; the things we valued in life had changed. We had both grown up, and through that process, our ideals changed along with our perspective on life and living. He was content with the wife, kids, job, and house achievements, but I wanted more. We loved each other, but were no longer in love. We were roommates, and I didn't want my kids growing up thinking this was what marriage was supposed to be like or that they had to live their lives inside the box of what society told them was appropriate.

I felt caged, and at the same time, felt the pull and desire for new and exciting things. I didn't have words to describe what I was yearning for, and I don't think I even knew what I wanted other than something more. I was far from content; I knew there was more to life. I wanted freedom. I wanted to be set free from this expectation of doing the expected—stay in my marriage and die a slow death, always wanting and needing more, and knowing there was more to life than what I was living.

After ten years of marriage, I was divorced at the age of twenty-nine. This was the first time I had ever lived alone. The kids would live with me one week, and their dad the next. My goal at this point was to focus on my kids and experience being alone. It was a struggle to adjust to this new way of living. The hardest part was learning how to balance being with my kids one week and not the next.

After adjusting to the week-on-week-off with the kids, I began to feel what freedom was like. During the weeks my kids were with their dad, I imagine I felt like most kids do when they go away to college for the first time: no parents, no rules. Although I had lived for ten years away from my parents and their rules, I had never experienced a time free of the expectations that come with living with another human being. I could dance around my house naked if I wanted, I could eat whatever I wanted when I wanted it, I could leave the dishes piled in the sink, I could arrange the furniture and decorate any way I wanted, and I didn't have to care if anyone else approved. I could do whatever I wanted, whenever and however I wanted, and answer to no one. This freedom became an addiction, and with any addiction comes poor choices.

A year after divorcing, I decided to start dating again. There is a whole set of bad choices that came along with that decision, but the poor choices I made from my addiction to freedom came at the expense of my kids. I regret the choices I made that hurt them. I was a really good mom before my freedom addiction, after which I seriously failed in motherhood, and the feeling of freedom became a drug to me.

It was never a question of whether I loved my children or not. I had and have a deep love for them, and they make me proud more than they know. I have to give credit to their dad and my parents for picking up the slack I created. They set good examples, made sure the kids' needs were met, and were there for them when they cried because their mother didn't do what she said she would do, or when they felt like I didn't love them anymore because I had chosen other things over them. They still lived with me every other week, but I was distracted, and they felt like a burden. I knew what I was doing, but couldn't stop without feeling like my freedom was being taken away again, and I was enabled to continue because their dad and my parents were there picking up the pieces.

Usually, kids grow out of the stage when they experience freedom from parents and rules for the first time, eventually realizing rules serve a purpose, and that freedom comes with great responsibility. For me, however, I have never seemed to outgrow that stage completely. I know rules serve a purpose, but I have never been a rule follower, per se, and I will question authority.

I no longer use freedom as a drug, but now experience freedom through adventure. I need to wonder, wander, and roam. I need to engage my curiosity and passion by experiencing undiscovered places, learning the untold mysteries of life, and walking the unpaved paths. It's a pilgrimage of self-discovery and growth for me. I can embrace those needs now and know that is how I was created, whether by nature or nurture.

Bad chapters can still create exceptional stories. Wrong paths can still lead to the right places. Failed dreams can still create successful people. Sometimes it takes losing yourself to find yourself.

I have attempted to heal from childhood trauma that made experiencing freedom for the first time such a powerful and potent drug for me.

I have tried to make amends for all the hurt and pain I caused my children. Society says it's our job as parents to raise good kids, but quite often, it's our children who teach us about life and how to live it. Fortunately, my kids seem to have escaped relatively unscathed by my shortcomings. They are both emotionally and physically happy and healthy individuals who show me better ways of living.

I have attempted to forgive myself, something I continue to attempt every day. Forgiving myself will be part of my lifelong journey, and I get better at it every day.

I am a free-spirited, adventurous wanderer who loves my freedom.

12

"She was a gypsy, as soon as you unraveled the many layers to her wild spirit she was on her next quest to discover her magic. She was relentless like that, the woman didn't need no body but an open road, a pen and a couple of sunsets."
—Nikki Rowe

You are full of energy and want to live life on your own terms, always open to change and embracing chaos. You have fire in your soul.

It was around 2014 when I started to hear about tiny houses and tiny house communities. I instantly loved the idea. I already knew I loved tiny spaces, and I'm the complete opposite of a claustrophobic; I feel safe in small, confining areas. I didn't need all the space

I had. When you have empty space, you just fill it up, and I don't like collecting things around my house that I don't use or need. So, living tiny is a perfect way of living for me. You can live with less stuff if you challenge yourself.

I found and started following The Village of Wildflowers in Flat Rock, North Carolina, on Facebook. Their tiny house community was just getting started, and I was curious to watch the progress. During my road trip in 2016, I was coming down through the eastern states along the coast and asked if anyone suggested points of interest I should stop at. A friend suggested Asheville, North Carolina, but I realized it was on the other side of North Carolina from my route. I wrote it off because it was way off course. But before I had headed too far south, I realized The Village of Wildflowers was in North Carolina, which hadn't registered in my mind because I was just following the page; I had no intention of ever going there. Once I knew how close the community was to Asheville, I changed course and skipped going through West Virginia so that I could visit Asheville and The Village of Wildflowers.

I really didn't care about going to Asheville so much as I wanted to see the tiny house community! Asheville was just an excuse so I didn't have to tell anyone I changed course just to visit a tiny house community. Even though I had set foot outside of the box society said I should be in, I wasn't going to step both feet out—at least, not yet!

I fell in love with the whole community and could picture myself living there one day. Visiting made me think of looking for other tiny house communities to see along the way. I visited a couple in Colorado, but they were nothing like the one in North Carolina. I continued to watch, more intently, the progress of the community in North Carolina and started to talk more about my idea. By some point in 2017, moving to the tiny house community in North Carolina became part of my three-to-five-year plan. Later, the goal became more specific, and I aimed for the summer of 2020. By then, my daughter would have completed two years of college, probably not want to live in a dorm anymore, and possibly have a place of her own. I thought by then I wouldn't feel like I was running out on my kids.

No one really questioned me about my goal. How many people talk about goals they never achieve, much less a harebrained one like this? It was someday in the future, and we all know someday never actually comes. But the more I talked about my goal, the more my daughter considered that it might actually happen. She was the only one who expressed concern, and her concern was more about what I was moving into rather than the idea of a tiny house community. She had never seen a tiny house or a community of tiny houses before. Seeing photos doesn't provide the full perspective; all she could picture was me moving to a trailer park. So, I decided to plan a trip during the summer of 2018 so I could take my daughter to see The Village of Wildflowers for herself and understand why I would move halfway across the country to live in this community. I had booked a night for us to stay in an actual tiny house within the community. Once she saw it for herself, she understood the attraction I had.

While sitting in the sales office of what is now called The Village at Simple Life, I was expressing my desire to move there in the summer of 2020 and asking what I needed to do to prepare, when I should buy, and what considerations I should make, etc. Unexpectedly, my daughter said, "Mom, you would love it here. I'm sure I won't come home from college as much as I think I will; you should just buy one." I sat for a moment in shock, but once I realized I had heard correctly, I didn't want to wait for her to take her words back. I was thrilled! I was thrilled I had her blessing, thrilled I was achieving my goal sooner than expected, and thrilled I was buying a tiny house.

The ball started rolling right then and there. We returned home, and I prepared to sell my house and most of my belongings. I lived in a 1,700-square-foot house full of furniture and belongings that wouldn't fit in my Chevy Trailblazer. I only took with me what would fit in my vehicle; that was it! No U-Haul, no trailer, only what fit in the vehicle. Even my little seven-pound dog jumped in while I was packing to make sure there was room left for him. I was so full of energy during this time. I was on fire with excitement and anticipation!

Changing the course of my life, parting with furniture and stuff, figuring out all the logistics of moving to another state, preparing my kids and family for this life change—it was surreal. It was full of chaos, full of so much change, and it was one of the most exciting times in my life!

According to Dr. Glenn Patrick Doyle, our brains are wired to keep us alive. Exposure to chaos and unpredictability in early life translates into preferring the pain we know rather than the danger we don't know. I would have to agree to a certain point. Chaos and unpredictability are what I learned to survive in, so it is familiar.

I was ready for this move! In a way, it was kind of like a fairy tale: the girl packs up her SUV with everything she owns, kisses her grown children and family goodbye, and heads out with her dog for a new beginning in a new state, halfway across the country! I never in my wildest dreams thought this would be me—that I would be the one moving across the country to a place I'd only been to twice! I didn't know a soul—not one being. I could work doing taxes from anywhere, so having my own tax prep business wasn't an issue. I would no longer have a mortgage, only rent for the lot my new house would occupy. It was so far from what the world expects a mom to do—ever—much less when her kids are eighteen and twenty-one. My daughter started college in August 2018, and I moved into a tiny house in North Carolina in September 2018. Usually, the kids grow up and go off to college, but instead, the mom grew up and moved away! The chronicle of my life has been change and chaos, both of which I thrive in. I want to live a simple yet authentic life.

Life is messy. Life changes constantly; you just may not acknowledge it. Life is chaotic at times. You can embrace the change and chaos and learn to swim through it, or drown in it. I choose to swim!

If you grew up with baby boomer parents, they might have worked at the same place for much of their lifetimes. It was not unusual to hear of people retiring from a company after forty years of service. I'm from Generation X. Although statistically, we don't necessarily stay at jobs as long as baby boomers, we are not known as job hoppers; that title is reserved for the later generations. I wouldn't call myself a job hopper, but I don't fall into the Gen X norm either. I have worked in so many different fields that it is hard to follow my resume. I have skills and strengths across the board. I'm adaptable and love the fact that I have done so many different things and have so many experiences.

My first job out of high school was with a temp agency that

offered office job placements. I was supposed to be heading to college, so I didn't want a regular job that I would have to leave after a brief time. I loved this job. Just due to this job alone, I piled up experiences. I was exposed to so many different industries and environments. After several months, I was placed with a company as a technical repair clerk, which turned into a full-time job. I worked there until after my son was born.

I tried for a year to be a stay-at-home mom, but I soon realized I was not special enough of a person to do that; I needed something more stimulating. But I had a tough time with the idea of leaving my baby. So, I got a job at a daycare working with four-and five-year-olds. I was able to bring my baby with me and stop in and see him whenever I wanted. It was good for him, and it was good for me. But before long, I was over all that. I decided it was time for me to get a job that was more suited for me—something I could make into a career.

I had no college degree and a gap in my work history, and I was twenty-two years old. I started a job in the mailroom of a bank. I loved my job. I felt so grown up, like an adult. It wasn't long before I was offered a promotion. I declined right away. I had read the policy manual and knew you had to be in a position for a minimum of six months before you could transfer to another position. They were kind enough to tell me that rule was for people who opted to transfer to a new position themselves, not for someone whom they chose to offer a new position. I happily learned that when you are an adult, rules are not necessarily set in stone, but made to be broken.

I ended my career at the bank ten years later in the executive offices. I had always been in some sort of administrative position during my time there. Still, I was part of so many different areas, including general services, facilities repair and maintenance, bank equipment, retail banking, auditing, finance, and more. I was afforded so many different opportunities. I was even named Sales Support Person of the Year one year.

While still in high school, I did telemarketing, worked at Burger King and grocery stores, and waitressed. Besides my bank job, I have done sales for Premier Design Jewelry and PartyLite Candles, worked at a floral shop, cleaned out rental houses, worked in residential construction, a medical office, and at an Amazon fulfillment center, and have been part of the event staff for numerous concerts and events. I have owned my own tax business since 2008. I have also been a realtor, and I taught tax classes. I was a district manager for a tax chain, worked for Intuit TurboTax, and did merchandising for Hershey's Chocolate. And yet I still would not call myself a job hopper!

Have you ever done something and then regretted it? We all have. But have you done something more permanent that you wish you wouldn't have done? A lot of us have done that too.

When I was a sophomore in high school, the cool new thing was getting a tattoo. I wanted one. I felt it was a rebellious thing to do. When I was sixteen, my friend and I ended up at a tattoo parlor. I didn't know you had to be eighteen or have parental consent, so I did not get a tattoo that night. They didn't require a parent to be present; a note giving permission was just fine. We returned a few nights later with a note my friend wrote, giving me permission and signed by her as my mom. They didn't even look at the note or read it; they just needed it for liability.

Tattoo shops in the early '90s were not like they are today. It was a little hole-in-the-wall shop that was probably not very clean, but I didn't care at the time. I was going to get a tattoo, and no one was stopping me. A large biker-looking man took my friend and me to this back room closed off by a red velvet curtain. I had picked a design of a pretty rose with wings. To this day, I have no idea why I thought that was cool or pretty. He drew the design on my chest, just down from my collarbone. He asked how it looked. It was smaller than I expected, but that was the size I could get for the money I was paying. I said it looked fine, and his tattoo gun buzzed away. I cut off the circulation in my friend's hand from squeezing it so tightly. I was scared it was going to hurt. It did, but not like I imagined it would. After it was outlined, it almost felt numb, so it was tolerable.

He was done quickly. I looked down, and it was not the colors I expected, but I didn't care. I had just rebelled. For whatever reason, tattoos are addictive. I got another tattoo a year later, at seventeen, with another note my friend scribed. After collecting a total of six tattoos, I have left that phase of my life. I don't want them anymore. The rose with wings I had covered up with a butterfly years later. I have a heart with tears on my ankle, a saying on my foot, a dandelion on my upper arm, a saying on my back shoulder, and my kids' names on the back of my forearm.

Several years ago, I started having them removed—all except my kids' names. Holy moly, does it hurt to have them removed by laser! And it costs a whole lot more than it did to get them! It's a process too. I have had five or six sessions on each of them, and none of them are gone. My first one, which was made into a butterfly, shows when I'm wearing certain dresses or tops, and I just don't like that. Since it was a cover-up, there is so much ink in that one; it will take a few more sessions than usual. The heart with tears on my ankle is almost gone and will probably be what I consider good enough after one more laser treatment.

The saying on my foot (*Even baby steps move you forward*) was really important to me at one time in my life and is still a good saying, but I just don't want it anymore. I am past the point in my life where I need that saying as a constant reminder. That has been the most painful one to have removed. I have an extremely high pain tolerance, but I have to make them stop every few letters. I have to take pain meds too; that's how bad that one hurt. It doesn't even look that different after multiple sessions.

I love dandelions, but the colors and design of it on my upper shoulder were not quite how I wished it would have turned out. That one is taking a bit to remove as well. Most of the color is gone at this point, but the ink was tattooed too deep, and my skin is actually scarred from the tattoo. You can feel the tattoo just by touching my arm, and will still be able to even when it's no longer visible.

The one on my back shoulder was my favorite, but I couldn't see it, and I made that fused glass plate to replicate it, so that one is almost gone now too. I don't necessarily regret any of my tattoos, but I am glad I can make changes, even if those changes are painful.

I am full of energy and want to live life on my own terms. I am always open to change. I embrace chaos and have fire in my soul!

13

"You say you love the rain, but you open your umbrella. You say you love the sun, but you find a shadow spot. You say you love the wind, but you close your window. This is why I am afraid; you say that you love me too."
—William Shakespeare

You are afraid to fall in love, but you love unconditionally.

Love is elusive and illusive to me. Something elusive avoids being caught, either physically by someone pursuing it or mentally by someone trying to understand it. Something illusive is based on an illusion, on something that is not true or real. That is a conundrum if there ever was one! I long to love and be loved, but my firsthand experiences with romantic love have not been the best. Being a sexual abuse survivor made me severely jaded in how I learned to define and express love. I hate the fact that the deepness of my love has been manipulated, mishandled, and misunderstood in the past, causing me to be fearful of loving and trusting now.

I grew up in a very loving home with a mom and dad who both loved me and each other very much. I had a family that I would say was pretty normal as far as families go in expressing our love for one another. Had I only experienced love from the perspective of my own family, I would view love in a much healthier way. But evil also exists in the world, and the decade-long abuse I endured wreaked perpetual havoc on me and my life. It skewed my understanding of what love is and how it is expressed. This, along with all the other physical, mental, and emotional damage from being abused for such a long time, affects how I live my life.

Of course, your programming can be changed, but it is hard, arduous work, and it is something you battle with, often silently, for a lifetime. Without being intentionally conscious of what you are thinking and doing, your mind just reverts to the path of least resistance—the paths your brain developed as you matured. This is why love is both elusive and illusive to me.

Traditionally, I have chosen unsafe people to be romantically involved with. I am not a good judge of character and have not trusted my intuition when I should have. I have hope that allows me to defend the actions of people whose behavior doesn't match their words. I romanticize situations and fall for potential rather than accepting reality. I desire to rescue people, to save them from themselves because they will change if they just have someone who loves them properly, right? *Nope.* That was a hard lesson to learn.

It's natural for people to be drawn to familiarity; it feels safe, even when it's not. Good feels bad, and bad feels familiar. I also deny my pain and perceptions. I would rather take on someone else's pain myself than watch them suffer. This is a disservice to them and me, but it's a pattern I have fallen into, and plenty of people out there are happy to pass their pain on to you.

Choosing love is a beautiful act of courage. We are not what we became when we were most afraid. We are what flows through us when we are most joyful and inspired. We are what we feel when everything feels at ease. We are what we know when that quiet little voice inside tells us it's going to be okay. We are not the person we became to cope with the life we didn't ask for. We are the person we choose to become in the life we build despite it.

Recovery from anything is liberating. It's a mindset change to become the kind of person you want to be. Every step of the way, you have to ask yourself if this is moving you or will move you closer to the real you. You must be open-minded about learning things about yourself. Even if it's painful, it's a step in the right direction toward becoming your best self. The Bible says in Genesis 50:20, "You intended to harm me, but God intended it for good to accomplish what is now being done, the saving of many lives."

It has taken me years of repeated patterns and heartache to realize these things about myself. The realization alone does not change anything. Change is hard, breaking patterns is hard, and figuring out how to do things differently is hard. You have to be intentional each and every day, and we all get tired and lazy sometimes.

It feels like healing myself from this has been a lesson I can't learn. But I refuse to fail and will spend my lifetime searching myself until I get it right. I don't want to be broken anymore; I don't want to be afraid to love; I will find love one day; I know this to be true.

Trauma is not something we just get over. Every cell of our body changes to adapt and survive and sees the self and the world through a sense of survival and danger. Children don't know the difference. Children become adults who unconsciously romanticize not being valued and seen, not because it's healthy, but because it feels safe.

I am afraid to fall in love, but I love unconditionally. I am working on this.

14

"I am a lover of words and tragically
beautiful things, poor timing
and longing, and all things with soul,
and I wonder if that means
I am entirely broken,
or if those are the things
that have been keeping me whole."

–Nicole Lyons

My Gypsy Soul Discovered

I've struggled with my purpose in life for so many years. I've always known God will use the events of my life as part of his purpose for me, but it's never been clear how. I thought it might be writing about my traumas or speaking about them. I know that might be a piece of it, but nothing has ever made clear sense. I would beat myself up because I couldn't figure out what I wanted in life. As soon as I thought I had figured it out, I'd realize that wasn't it and wonder what was next.

This term, *gypsy soul*, started a fire in me, and I felt like I began to understand a part of myself I've always tried to extinguish. Now I can embrace it, continue to understand it, and figure out how it defines my life.

If you are not a gypsy soul, you are satisfied with an annual vacation. I never seem to be satisfied. There is always more out there—more experiences, more places, more life to be lived. My soul is asking me to let go of all I've ever known so I can receive all I've ever asked for.

You can be afraid and brave at the exact same time. Being afraid is not the same as being scared. Scared means being in a state of fear, nervousness, or panic. Generally, I am not those things, but I can sometimes feel afraid, which means feeling fear or apprehension. I can face my fear and do it anyhow! I will fail at times. I will get it wrong occasionally. I will take two steps back once in a while, but as long as I don't stay there and I can bravely take a step forward again, I will be on my way to wherever my journey leads me.

We think we will learn who we are or discover our purpose while we travel or experience new things. Those things can be life-changing, but I didn't discover who I was during my road trip or my move across the country. I learned who I was on an ordinary day while driving to work and listening to the radio.

It's a process, a journey, and I have become aware of just how much my gypsy soul has been sneaking out without me even knowing. When I moved to North Carolina in the fall of 2018 to live in a tiny house community, I thought that would be my forever home. I thought I'd figured it out and would be where I wanted to be and wouldn't have any desire to do something different. But then I realized that in the four short years since my move, I have moved around nine different times! That doesn't even include my ten-month stint living in a motorhome where I changed locations a total of five times, each time in a different state. None of these moves were really planned, but when opportunity knocked, I answered! Some moves were due to life changes, others due to necessity, but nonetheless, they were changes I willingly accepted.

Writing is my self-care, my way to process, learn, discover, and remember. Writing this book has been a profound experience. I wonder where my journey will wander from here! I've come to enjoy going with the flow. I am letting the chips fall where they may. Stay tuned.

Latcho drom!

Acknowledgments

Life is so much better when you have a village to rely on that supports you, even when they think you are crazy! My village has changed over the years, but when someone new comes into your village, you never know what their particular purpose will be in your story. Even if they are only there for a season, they can create a ripple that lasts a lifetime.

My favorite boss gave me a nugget of wisdom that has stayed with me. (He actually gave me many nuggets that I refer to as Larry Lessons!) Part of my job at the time was creating, and whether it was correspondence, systems, processes, or procedures, Larry would always change something! One day, I was feeling defeated by all the changes he was making to what I had done. He told me, "It's easier to criticize than to create." This phrase eternally changed my perspective. It has come in handy during so many situations, even more so when drafting a book. Thank you, Larry, for the ripple you created all those years ago when you said something to me that you probably don't even remember saying! Never underestimate the power of words.

I have so much appreciation for the current tribe in my village. You have loved me, supported me, encouraged me, and made my crazy feel acceptable!

Many people went into making this book a reality. Thank you to Carole, Mary Beth, and Sherry; your insights were helpful.

Tamara, you were the first to read the entire manuscript in one sitting! Your perspective was insightful and encouraging. Thank you.

Tessa, I knew from the first time we met and the words you used that we are soul sisters! Your excitement, passion, and praise have been such a blessing. Our paths were meant to cross.

Kaycee, you have seen the good and the bad. You lived part of this journey with me, and I am forever grateful for our friendship!

Paula, you have been in the passenger seat for this whole ride. You are an excellent navigator and knew where I was going sometimes before I knew myself. Your encouragement and direction were always spot on!

Mom and Rick, I couldn't have made it to where I am today without all your love, guidance, and support. Words can't express the gratitude I feel for you. Thank you for loving me no matter who I am.

My editors, Carmen Riot Smith and Robin Fuller, thank you for what you each did in making my book better. Carmen, your words to me after your edit made me happy-cry, something I never do; I typically only cry at sad things! You have been a source of encouragement for me in seeing my vision. Robin, I appreciate your attention to every detail and your gift of small changes that make such huge differences.

Most importantly, God's grace is sufficient for me, and his power is made perfect in my weakness. To him be all the glory.

About the Author

Catina Borgmann is a free-spirited, adventurous woman who has discovered and subsequently embraced her authentic gypsy soul. She was born and raised in Nebraska and lived there until 2018, when she followed her dream to live in a tiny house community in North Carolina.

Catina is a catalyst for self-love, self-discovery, and living an authentic life. Along the way, she has made mistakes, learned lessons, fought battles, won victories, survived traumas, become an author, and started a blog. She's managed to always find joy within her journeys.

Through her company, GypsyWander, she hopes to inspire and encourage free-spirited women around the world to live authentically and find joy in their own journeys. You can find her at **www.GypsyWander.life**, on Facebook, and on Pinterest.